# IS~~SUES~~

# 2000

*Evangelical Faith & Cultural Trends
in the New Millennium*

■ ■ ■ ■ ■ ■ ■ ■ ■ ■ ■ ■ ■ ■ ■ ■ ■ ■ ■ ■ ■ ■ ■ ■ ■ ■ ■

# MAL COUCH
## General Editor

kregel
PUBLICATIONS

Grand Rapids, MI 49501

*Issues 2000: Evangelical Faith & Cultural Trends in the New Millennium*

Published in 1999 by Kregel Publications, a division of Kregel, Inc., P.O. Box 2607, Grand Rapids, MI 49501. Kregel Publications provides trusted, biblical publications for Christian growth and service. Your comments and suggestions are valued.

For more information about Kregel Publications, visit our web site: www.kregel.com

Cover design: Nicholas G. Richardson
Book design: Frank Gutbrod

All views expressed in this work are solely those of the authors and do not represent or reflect the position or endorsement of any governmental agency or department, military or otherwise.

**Library of Congress Cataloging-in-Publication Data**
Couch, Mal.
    Issues 2000: evangelical faith and cultural trends in the new millennium / by Mal Couch.
       p.    cm.
    Includes bibliographical references.
    1. Christianity and culture—History—20th century.
2. Christianity—20th century.     I. Title.
 II. Title: Issues two thousand.
BR115.C8C635   1999   230'.04624—dc21    99-19008
                                           CIP

ISBN 0-8254-2363-5

Printed in the United States of America

1 2 3 4 5 / 03 02 01 00 99

# TABLE OF CONTENTS

# CONTRIBUTORS

**Mal Couch**, M.A., Th.M., Th.D., Ph.D., is founder and president of Tyndale Theological Seminary and Biblical Institute in Fort Worth, Texas. He is general editor of several books, including the popular *Dictionary of Premillennial Theology* and *A Biblical Handbook to the Acts of the Apostles*.

**Timothy J. Demy**, M.A., Th.M., Th.D., Ph.D. candidate, is a military chaplain and adjunct instructor at the U.S. Naval War College, Newport, Rhode Island. He is the author, coauthor, and editor of numerous books and articles on theology, ethics, and history, including *Genetic Engineering: A Christian Response*.

**Paul R. Fink**, Th.D., is chairman of the Department of Biblical Studies and serves as professor of biblical studies and pastoral ministry at Liberty University, Lynchburg, Virginia.

**Thomas Ice**, Th.M, Ph.D., an author and conference speaker, is executive director of the PreTrib Research Center. His works include *Fast Facts on Bible Prophecy*, *When the Trumpet Sounds*, and *The Coming Cashless Society*.

**Tim LaHaye**, D.Min., is president and founder of Family Life Seminars. He is a minister, public speaker, television/radio commentator, and the author of nearly three dozen books, including *How to Study the Bible for Yourself* and the Left Behind series (coauthored with Jerry Jenkins).

**David A. Noebel**, B.A., M.A., Ph.D. candidate, is co-founder and president of Summit Ministries in Manitou Springs, Colorado. He is the author of numerous articles and books, including *Understanding the Times* and *Clergy in the Classroom*.

**Gary P. Stewart**, M.Div., Th.M., M.A., D.Min. candidate, is a military chaplain based in the Chicago area. He is coauthor and editor of numerous books, including the BioBasics series and *Genetic Engineering: A Christian Response*.

# INTRODUCTION: WHY THIS BOOK?

Between 1910 and 1915, a series of essays explaining biblical Christian doctrines appeared; it was entitled *The Fundamentals*. The series was "a testimony to the truth" by a group of conservative Bible scholars who felt the winds of liberal untruth blowing upon the world and the church. They believed that it was vital to restate what was most important to the continuation of Christian faith.

Several developments led to their fears. Most had to do with German critical theories and the social gospel, both of which were eroding belief in the inspiration and inerrancy of Scripture. Among modernists the Bible had no authority. The virgin birth, resurrection, and atonement of Christ for sins were doubted or denied in pulpits and seminary classrooms. *The Fundamentals* reminded Christians of their roots and alerted a new generation to the relevance of the Word of God to current issues.

The need again seems compelling for a panoramic sweep of biblical truth by godly Bible teachers. Our purpose has been to restate the truths that cannot be compromised and to speak to the generations now reaching adulthood with the dawn of the new century. *The Fundamentals* were remarkable works that to some degree guided the church through a dark period of the early twentieth century. A restatement is needed as a guide into tomorrow.

Thirty-two authors and Bible teachers have contributed to a comprehensive collection that will be coming from Kregel Publications in the spring of 2000, *The Fundamentals for the Twenty-First Century*. Meanwhile, we felt it important to produce a smaller version to address specifically those issues that other generations did not face. Our message: The Bible speaks to us now as well, in fundamental truths we dare not ignore.

Seven chapters that also will appear in *The Fundamentals for the Twenty-First Century* have been chosen to warn us all of impending

7

moral and spiritual disasters that may lead into deepening darkness and apostasy.

David Noebel describes godless new philosophical beliefs that directly challenge the Scriptures. Timothy Demy shows how technology blesses and curses those it is meant to serve. Technology can blind us to the supernatural; it can and does even replace God in many lives. Thomas Ice describes a popular mysticism that undercuts the principles of biblical spirituality.

Tim LaHaye and Paul Fink warn America of the danger of losing the national soul. They challenge Christians to consider how the state already looks on the church as its enemy. Soon a modern wave of Western persecution may come to Christians in North America. Gary Stewart continues this theme, commenting on the new intolerant demands for tolerance. Christians already are out of step with society and may be dealt with harshly.

The studies conclude with an examination of spiritual apostasy and how the Bible describes the ultimate hope—the rapture of the church—whatever else the future holds.

The twenty-first century will be fraught with many spiritual, technological, and social dangers. *Issues 2000* and *The Fundamentals for the Twenty-First Century* are meant not only to warn but also to stabilize, doctrinally and spiritually. The contributors share a desire that today's generation and those of the future will be grounded in fundamental faith in Christ. This stability is what the Bible teaches, and it provides the only way to live in a Christless environment.

Peter reminds us:

> You therefore, beloved, knowing this beforehand, be on your guard lest being carried away by the error of unprincipled men, you fall from your own steadfastness. (2 Peter 3:17)

Mal Couch

# 1

# THE WORLDVIEWS OF DESTRUCTION IN THE TWENTIETH CENTURY

## David A. Noebel

> See to it that no one [educator, politician, musician, news anchor] takes you captive through philosophy and empty deception [naturalism, materialism, existentialism, hedonism, pragmatism], according to the tradition of men [Marx, Darwin, Nietzsche, Wellhausen, Freud, Dewey, Foucault], according to the elementary principles of the world [socialism, naturalistic evolution, higher criticism, humanism, moral relativism, deconstructionism, collectivism], rather than according to Christ. (Col. 2:8)

The twentieth century, to a great extent, has been the consummate setting for the practice of this text. Western civilization in general, and the United States in particular, has embarked on a hazardous journey of rejecting and replacing Christ with any number of mortal men and their ideas. Since ideas have consequences, the twentieth century has reaped the fruit of these utopian schemes and seemingly superior ideas. This chapter surveys the damage.

More than one hundred years ago (1890–1891), James Orr presented the Kerr lectures in Edinburgh, Scotland. He entitled his series "The Christian View of God and the World" and argued forcefully that biblical Christianity is a worldview (Ger. *Weltanschauung*). He meant that Christianity is more than a two-hour emotional experience on Sunday morning. Christianity is a twenty-four-hour-a-day view of reality based on a relationship with God through Jesus Christ.

The corollary to that proposition is that one who believes and commits to the belief that Jesus Christ is the Son of God is thereby committed to much else besides, said Orr. Christianity is more than heart. It is head as well. It is body, mind, soul, and spirit (see Mark 12:30). The Christian, by the very fact that he or she is a Christian, is committed to a "view of God, to a view of man, to a view of sin, to a view of redemption, to a view of the purpose of God in creation and history, to a view of human destiny."[1] Together these views add up to a worldview.

In another work, I define worldview as *any ideology, philosophy, theology, movement, or religion that provides an overarching approach to understanding God, the world, humans, and humanity's relations to God and the world.*[2] Specifically, a worldview expresses a particular perspective regarding each of the following ten areas: theology, philosophy, ethics, biology, psychology, sociology, law, politics, economics, and history.

Not surprisingly, the worldviews of destruction in the twentieth century injected their ideas into these areas, but they were ideas responsible for the death of millions. That is the subject of this chapter.

At approximately the same time that James Orr penned his work, four other individuals (three men and one woman) were about to emerge on the world's stage. Before they finished speaking, writing, and living out their worldviews, millions of people would lose their lives. And as we enter the twenty-first century, millions more will perish because of these same worldviews and the ideas they contain.

The twentieth century is now history. It is a history of incredible advances in inventions, computer chips, medical science, technologies, transportation, communications, expansion of the Christian gospel, living standards, and the number of free governments, but devolution in dictatorships, poverty, illegal drugs, pornography, homosexuality, sexually transmitted diseases—particularly HIV—lawlessness, immorality, teenage pregnancy, and abortion. Most to the point here, it is a century of murder unequaled in history. The twentieth century was the century of slaughter. More people have been killed by violence at the hands of others during the twentieth century than in all previous centuries combined.

During the first eighty-eight years of the twentieth century, says historian R. J. Rummel:

> almost 170 million men, women and children have been shot, beaten, tortured, knifed, burned, starved, frozen, crushed or worked to death; buried alive, drowned, hung, bombed, or killed in any other of the myriad ways governments have inflicted death on unarmed, helpless citizens and foreigners. The dead could conceivably be nearly 360 million people. It is as though our species has been devastated by a modern Black Plague. And indeed it has, but a plague of Power, not germs.[3]

When we put the human cost of war and genocide together, says Rummel, "power has killed over 203 million people in this century,"[4] and this figure does not include the slaughter of the innocent (abortion)—a foundation stone of the secular humanist worldview—or those slaughtered during the final twelve years of the twentieth century.

These millions did not die because of James Orr's Christian worldview. Most of these millions died at the ideological hands of the three men and one woman whose worldviews inflicted the world. The three men are Benito Mussolini (1883–1945), Adolph Hitler (1889–1945), and Josef Stalin (1879–1953). The woman is Margaret Sanger (1883–1966). Mussolini and Hitler represent the twentieth century's fascist/Nazi worldviews; Stalin represents the Marxist/Leninist worldview; Sanger represents the secular humanist worldview.

These are the worldviews primarily responsible for the millions who have been slaughtered on the altars of atheism, naturalism, dialectical materialism, ethical relativism, libertinism, class morality, biological evolution, social Darwinism, euthanasia, sterilization, infanticide, eugenics, abortion, collectivism, statism, dictatorship, new fascist man, new Aryan man, new soviet man, new humanist man, new international child of the future, new social order, new world order, socialism (national and international), positive law or sociological jurisprudence, and other ideas from the fevered brows of the intelligentsia.

In his 1948 social commentary by that title, social historian Richard Weaver summarized the twentieth century with his observation that "Ideas have consequences." The ideas that were sown in the nineteenth century were reaped in the twentieth, and the results should be obvious for all to see—death, destruction, devastation, heartache, misery; all words and nuances that portray a century ripe for judgment.

As we begin century twenty-one, we have yet to admit a dark secret: The ideas that brought us a century of terror and slaughter are still being taught in our public institutions of lower and higher education. Ironically, the only worldview not responsible for the slaughter is the only worldview proscribed: biblical Christianity. All other worldviews have their voices and defenders in our colleges and universities.

"Paul DeMan," for example, says Gene Edward Veith Jr., "who has done more than anyone else to promote deconstruction in the United States, was a Nazi propagandist."[5] Michel Foucault, a major postmodern voice and lecturer at the University of California (Berkeley) was a Maoist[6] and a homosexual who died of AIDS after infecting his lovers with the purpose of "inventing new pleasures beyond sex . . . sex as murder."[7]

And who can deny that both Friedrich Nietzsche (1844–1900) and Martin Heidegger (1889–1976) are "back in fashion on university campuses."[8] Nietzsche was not only a major precursor to fascism, but is openly admitted to be the father of postmodernism. Heidegger was an active, ideologically committed member of the Nazi party.[9]

The Marxist influence on America's campuses is also rampant as Arnold Beichman notes in *The Weekly Standard*. America's communists and former communists are already taking out full-page ads in the *New York Times* seeking to exculpate communism. Historian Theodore Draper is quoted as saying:

> Clearly an attempt to rehabilitate Communism by making it part of the larger family of socialism and democracy is underway. No one would think of doing this favor for fascism, but Communism with even more millions of victims and a much longer life span is the beneficiary of this sustained effort of historical rehabilitation in—of all places—American colleges and universities.[10]

David Horowitz reminisces in his autobiography:

> The situation in the universities was appalling. The Marxists and socialists who had been refuted by historical events were now the tenured establishment of the academic world. Marxism had produced the bloodiest and most oppressive regimes in human history—but after the fall, as one wit commented, more Marxists could

be found on the faculties of American colleges than in the entire former Communist bloc. The American Historical Association was run by Marxists, as was the professional literature association.[11]

And in America, one worldview practically monopolizes public education. It is the worldview of Sanger and John Dewey (1859–1952), the worldview of thousands of professors and teachers and entertainers and professional organizations. It is the secular humanist worldview. "The [secular] humanistic system of values has now become the predominant way of thinking in most of the power centers of society," says James C. Dobson and Gary L. Bauer.[12] Dobson specifically mentions the universities, the news media, the entertainment industry, the judiciary, the federal bureaucracy, the public schools, and Congress. Elsewhere Dobson and Bauer state that "professors, whose salaries are paid by the taxes and tuition subsidies of millions of hard-working Americans, ridicule capitalism, attack family values, and rewrite American history, so that if it is taught at all, America is always the villain."[13]

The twentieth century was the century in which the humanistic worldview vigorously and systematically eradicated the biblical Christian worldview from the public square in the West.[14] If this continues into the twenty-first century, one can expect the same results—death and destruction.

## Nazism

What Christians, in the main, have not understood is that Nazism is a worldview. And since worldviews by definition contain a theology, Nazism is a religious worldview. There are no nonreligious worldviews. Most Christians look upon Nazism, fascism, and communism as being merely political and/or economic movements. And many Christians have missed the point that secular humanism is a worldview and therefore, by definition, a religious worldview. Contrary to some German Christians, who insisted that their Nazi government was "a state that once again rules in God's name," none of the ingredients of Nazism were Christian, or even theistic.[15] The philosophy is pagan with occult overtones. Deitrich Echart, for example, a founding member of the Nazi Party, was "a dedicated satanist, a man immersed in black magic and the Thule group of occultists." Heinrich Himmler (1900–1945), Alfred Rosenberg (1893–1946), and Paul Joseph Goebbels (1897–1945) were dedicated occultists, as was Karl Haushofer (1869–1946), who became Hitler's spiritual mentor following Echart's death. According to

Erwin Lutzer, Haushofer took Hitler "through the deepest levels of occult transformation."[16]

While Hitler embodied the Nazi worldview, behind him stood an assemblage of philosophers and theologians including DeMan, Heidegger, Nietzsche, Charles Darwin (1809–1882), Karl Marx (1818–1883),[17] Richard Wagner (1813–1883),[18] Karl Barth (1886–1968), and a "who's who" of intellectuals amongst Europe's elite. Veith relates, "The intellectual establishment itself is trying to keep hidden the fact that European high culture in its most advanced phase not only was powerless to prevent the construction and implementation of the death camps, but actually provided the ideological base on which the death camps were built."[19]

No matter how pagan, occultist, or even anti-Jewish or anti-Christian Nazism may have been, or how socialistic, collectivistic, or evolutionistic, on Easter Sunday, April 16, 1933, "Protestant pastors across Bavaria delivered an official blessing of Nazism . . . passed the collection plate on Hitler's birthday, beflagged their churches on state holidays, and even marched in the 1933 May Day Parade for National Labor with swastikas stitched to their Vestments."[20]

In fairness to these pastors, it should be noted that in 1918 Marxist Kurt Eisner staged a communist coup in Munich and held the city for over three months.[21] The Nazis played on a resulting fear of communism and insisted that Christianity and Nazism fight the "Red Terror" together.

What the pastors didn't realize was that Hitler's militant socialism and Marxist socialism are blood brothers—one national, one international—and that the Nazis were quick to adopt Soviet methods. They imported from Russia, according to Ludwig von Mises:

> the one-party system and the pre-eminence of this party in political life; the paramount position assigned to the secret police, the concentration camps; the administrative execution or imprisonment of all opponents; the extermination of the families of suspects and of exiles; the methods of propaganda; etc., etc. . . . There were nowhere more docile disciples of Lenin, Trotsky and Stalin than the Nazis were.[22]

University of Wisconsin historian Stanley G. Payne summarizes some of the major ingredients of Nazism. These include dictatorship, a new Social Darwinian structure of state and society, a racial revolution, and a state-regulated national socialism.[23]

A. E. Wilder-Smith in *Man's Origin, Man's Destiny* points up the two major ideas behind Hitler and his Nazi movement. Says Wilder-Smith: "It is noteworthy that many of our Western intellectuals have socialistic as well as Darwinian views. Perhaps the two positions may be related. But it is more remarkable that Darwinism is not only the state doctrine of the communists but was also that of the National Socialists and Fascists."[24]

Anyone reading Hitler's *Mein Kampf (My Struggle)* realizes the debt Hitler owed to naturalist evolution theory and how he based his racial and militaristic policies on the theories of Darwin and his successors. "Darwin's concepts of struggle for existence," says Wilder-Smith, "dominated Hitler's whole thinking and, by guiding selection in this struggle, Hitler intended to help nature a little."[25]

Certainly Darwinism is still taught throughout the world's colleges and universities.[26] It is also taught at the high school level with absolutely no competition since the U.S. Supreme Court ruled that creationism is unconstitutional and cannot be taught. The writer of that decision, Justice William Brennan, was the court's most vocal secular humanist.

This decision was made in the face of a comment by Cambridge professor Adam Sedgwick, after reading Darwin's *Origin of Species through Natural Selection or the Preservation of Favored Races in the Struggle for Life*: "If this book were to find general public acceptance, it would bring with it a brutalization of the human race such as it had never seen before."[27]

Can anyone seriously doubt that the twentieth century has witnessed the fulfillment of Sedgwick's observation as Hitler, Mussolini, and Stalin glorified struggle and war on the basis of the struggle for life?

Journalist and researcher Ian T. Taylor summarizes a number of scholars who "noted the strong connection between evolutionary theory and the German Führer's objectives." Taylor also points out that Werner Maser's study of Hitler found that "Darwin was the general source for Hitler's biology, worship, force, and struggle, and of his rejection of moral causality in history."[28]

Darwin wasn't Hitler's only god, however. Since the word *Nazi* means national socialism, it should not surprise anyone that socialism is as much a part of the Nazi worldview as is evolutionism.[29] Then, too, socialism is consistent with collectivism or statism since it requires a dictator to abolish or control private property and decide when to produce a pair of shoes.

Friedrich A. Hayek, in his book *The Road to Serfdom*, observed the mental collectivizing of students in Germany. He writes that "many a university professor during the 1930s has seen English and American students return from the continent uncertain whether they were communists or Nazis and certain only that they hated Western liberal (in the traditional sense) Civilization."[30]

Youth flocked to the Nazis and to communist causes, and some observed the incredible "susceptibility of university-trained people in Germany to totalitarian appeals."[31] Twenty-five percent of the Nazi SS officers had Ph.D degrees. Germany's intellectual community prepared the German people and especially the German youth for the "acceptance of some form of militant socialism."[32] Writers on socialism Richard Vetterli and William E. Fort Jr. quote Hans Kohn that "within little more than a decade German intellectuals succeeded in leading German people into the Abyss."[33] Kohn says that the philosophy of Heidegger, the political theory of Carl Schmitt, and the theology of Barth primarily convinced German intellectuals that Germany's future was not with the West.[34]

Barth, of course, joined forces with the anti-Nazi movement and signed the Barmen Declaration with other members of the independent Confessing Church movement, but as John Robbins notes, while Barth's theological views changed over the decades, his political and economic views did not. Barth admitted that he chose theology because he felt a need to find a better basis for his social action. He was referred to as "Comrade Pastor." He claimed that socialism "is a very important and necessary application of the gospel"[35]:

> If you understand the connection between the person of Jesus and your socialist convictions, and if you now want to arrange your life so that it corresponds to this connection, then that does not at all mean you have to "believe" or accept this, that, or the other thing. What Jesus has to bring us are not ideas, but a way of life. One can have Christian ideas about God and the world and about human redemption, and still with all that be a complete heathen. And as an atheist, a materialist, and a Darwinist, one can be a genuine follower and disciple of Jesus. Jesus is not the Christian worldview and the Christian worldview is not Jesus.[36]

Unfortunately for Barth and his defenders, he also ended up praising communism and even Joseph Stalin. He was the ultimate anti-anticommunist.[37]

So, it wasn't just the teachings of Heidegger, Marx, Nietzsche, and Johann Gottlieb Fichte (1762–1814) that prepared Germany for Hitler and Nazism; it was also Emanuel Hirsch, a dialectical theologian; Paul Tillich (1886–1965), a Marxist socialist theologian; and such respected men as Barth, Rudolf Bultmann (1884–1976), Friedrich Delitzsch (1813–1890), and Gerhard Kittel (1888–1948).[38] They all played a role in turning the hearts and minds of the German people away from Christ, the cross, the empty tomb, and biblical Christianity, to Darwinism, the national socialist movement, and, in some cases, Marxist socialism. For example, Hirsch, and those who basically accepted German higher criticism, taught that the resurrection of Jesus Christ was "only a spiritual vision" and that the resurrection accounts in the Gospels were later additions. Hirsch thought that the idea of a physical resurrection distorted Christianity by focusing attention on the hereafter instead of the present. He stressed the importance of community in the Christian life.[39] Tillich, a member of the Marxist Frankfurt School, was never friendly to biblical Christianity, and Bultmann advocated "demythologizing" the New Testament.[40]

In *Modern Fascism* Veith explains why Hitler and the Nazis were anti-Jewish. It was more than a view that Jews were an "inferior race." Hitler hated the worldview of the Jews—especially their monotheism and defense of an absolute moral order based on something apart from the natural order. Nazis believed that right and wrong are determined by nature, state, community, or choice. They rejected the notion of a God who judges according to His standards. Hitler regarded Bible-believing Christians as a subset of the Jews, and his antipathy toward both was as much theological as racial. Christians who believed the Bible generally rejected Hitler; those softened by German higher criticism generally collaborated with the German church. Hitler referred to the Christianity that submitted as "positive Christianity."[41]

We have not learned much from this portion of history, according to historian Franklin Littell:

> The lessons to be learned from the Church Struggle and the Holocaust have hardly penetrated our Protestant seminaries, our liberal Protestant press, our church literature, the thinking and writing of even our ablest older theologians. . . . American Liberal Protestantism is sick, and the theological form of its sickness can be summarized by saying that it stands solidly on ground but lately vacated by the "German Christians". . . who collaborated with Nazism.[42]

Today's so-called Jesus Seminar movement, along with the Third Quest movement, is merely a replay of the First and Second Quest movements that gave us the theological basis for the "isms" that brought terror on the twentieth century. First Quest David Frederick Strauss's *Life of Jesus* (1835) not only influenced Karl Marx but also the Jesus Seminar's scholarly unbelievers.[43] There is a huge volume of scholarship to support the picture of Christ that Matthew, Mark, Luke, and John portray. Yet skeptics and unbelievers in our institutions of higher education continue to undermine biblical Christianity and those who have faith in Jesus Christ.

## Fascism

Fascism is a worldview in the same vein as Nazism, and the terms are often used interchangeably in relation to the world political situation of the 1920s–1940s. It was a pagan religion with worship of the state and *Il Duce*.

Fascism, says Stanley G. Payne, was a product of the culture and social Darwinism of the early twentieth century. It usually accompanied a warrior spirit and a movement for fundamental international change. "Its pagan warrior mentality sometimes conflicted with the norms and processes of modernization, but fascist states eagerly incorporated major functions of rationalization and modern development."[44]

Evolution was as important to Mussolini as to Hitler. A. E. Wilder-Smith states that both "Hitler and Mussolini glorified struggle and war on the basis that the fittest would survive and the race would be thus cleansed."[45] Both sought to assist nature in its inexorable process of lifting mankind. Elsewhere Wilder-Smith says that Mussolini found "evolutionary doctrine a real windfall, in fact, a godsend." It gave Mussolini the excuse to enslave whole groups of people, or wipe them out—especially if they were less highly evolved than his own people. The whole concept of evolution, says Wilder-Smith, "justifies the terror of fascism, communism, and other types of tyranny."[46]

According to Veith, the elements of the fascist worldview emerged from three sources: romanticism, Darwinism, and existentialism. These were mainstream Western thought patterns, the assumptions of the intellectual elite during the 1930s. Fascist totalitarianism sought to control all of life and establish a new religion. Says Veith: "This new worldview defined itself against the existing spiritual framework—that of the Jews and their Bible. In rejecting not only the Bible but objective meaning, transcendent morality, and the authority of language itself, the fascists arrayed themselves against the Word."[47]

As Hitler, who failed the lower grades of high school but filled his quiver with intellectuals, Mussolini found support in some of the great modern thinkers and writers.[48] These included Ezra Pound, D. H. Lawrence, W. B. Yeats, George Bernard Shaw, Wyndham Lewis, T. E. Hulme, Roy Campbell, and T. S. Eliot (early in his career). In avant-garde art, fascist sympathizers were found among the vorticists, Italian futurists, and German expressionists.[49]

Shaw, founder of the socialist British Fabian Society, characterized the Jews as "the real enemy, the invader from the East, the Druze, the ruffian, the oriental parasite." Henri Bernstein, the French Jewish writer, sarcastically referred to Shaw as a "dear socialist, multimillionaire and anti-Semite." Shaw advised the Germans to "force the Jews to wed Aryans"; thus, he claimed, the Jewish question would be solved.[50]

Shaw's fascistic bent was coupled with intense communist sympathies. "All totalitarianism fascinated him since they fitted into his plans for a rigid collectivism." Therefore, he could announce to the world, "We, as socialists, have nothing to do with liberty. Our message, like Mussolini's, is one of discipline, of service, of ruthless refusal to acknowledge any natural right of competence."[51] His definition of socialism (though it is true also of fascism, Nazism, communism, and Fabianism[52]) was "You would be forcibly fed, clothed, lodged, taught and employed whether you liked it or not. If it were discovered that you had not character and industry enough to be worth all this trouble, you might possibly be executed in a kindly manner."[53]

None of these individuals or movements could be considered conservative in any meaningful sense of the word. The true situation was not one of socialism on the left wing and fascism on the right wing.[54] The word *conservative* implies limited government. Fascism, Nazism, and communism were brutal socialist dictatorships, and Mussolini's father was a socialist revolutionary, and Mussolini began in an orthodox Marxist position.[55] In fact, according to von Mises, "nobody could surpass Mussolini in Marxist zeal. He was the intransigent champion of the pure creed, the unyielding defender of the rights of the exploited proletarians, the eloquent prophet of the socialist bliss to come."[56] Mussolini was under the influence of an Angelica Balbanoff, a trained communist agent who was later to become the first secretary of the Third Communist International.[57] Mussolini also edited a socialist newspaper, *The Class Struggle*, and thought himself to be Nietzsche's "Superman."

Vetterli and Fort find that Mussolini exemplified much of the philosophy of Nietzsche:

> To Nietzsche, the will to power, the desire to dominate gave meaning to life. Truth is relative. It is freed from moral connotations. Truth is whatever aids the will to power. . . . This superman would be beyond the pale of moral restraint. He would himself create the standard of value. The cult of power was to replace traditional religion and moral values. There is no doubt that Benito Mussolini, (as Hitler after him) believed himself to be the personification of Nietzsche's superman.[58]

Have we learned anything from this portion of history? The instructions of Nazism are

1. will to power
2. define morality as relative
3. regard truth as relative
4. replace traditional religion
5. replace moral values

These are fundamental planks of postmodernism, the rage of the intellectuals on America's colleges and universities at the start of the twenty-first century.[59]

## *Marxism/Leninism*

The third destructive worldview of the twentieth century is Marxism/Leninism. Marxism is a well-developed atheistic, materialistic, evolutionistic, socialistic worldview.[60]

This worldview has been the greatest killing machine in recorded history. And history has recorded some unbelievable mass killings.[61]

Hitler has the distinction of eliminating 21 million people, but Lenin, Stalin, Mao Tse-tung, and other communist dictators have eliminated 80 million.[62] The suffering and stark terror of this figure is humanly impossible to comprehend. For a taste of what was involved, we recommend Robert Conquest's *Harvest of Sorrows*, the account of Stalin's slaughter of the Ukrainian people. Stalin's basis for such a slaughter was Darwin: "Evolution," said Stalin, "prepares for revolution and creates the ground for it; revolution consummates the process of evolution and facilitates its further activity."[63] The Ukrainians were considered not fit to survive! Before Stalin could move into the high stakes of death and destruction, however, he needed Marx and Lenin.

Marx wrote *The Communist Manifesto* in 1848, calling for elimination of the bourgeoisie (property owners). "This person [the bourgeois] must, indeed, be swept out of the way, and made impossible," he proclaimed.[64] "The Communists everywhere support every revolutionary movement against the existing social and political order of things."[65] "They [communists] openly declare that their ends can be attained only by the forcible overthrow of all existing social conditions."[66] Lenin took this one step further and set up the state apparatus to eliminate the bourgeoisie. And while Lenin did his fair share of killing, it was Joseph Stalin and Mao who took Marx's teachings and Lenin's state apparatus to its ultimate extent.

Again, as with Nazism and fascism, Marxist/Leninist/Stalinist communism is based on Darwinism, socialism, and statism. It is also based on atheism, dialectical materialism, and proletariat morality. In fact, the millions who perished at the hands of the communists perished under the innocent-sounding expression of proletariat morality. The bourgeoisie were unfit to live since they believed in God, believed in a created order, believed in transcendent morality, believed in family values, believed in owning property, and so forth.

"It is a commonplace," says Jacques Barzun, "that Marx felt his own work to be the exact parallel of Darwin's. He even wished to dedicate a portion of *Das Kapital* to the author of *The Origin of Species*."[67]

Marx thought that he had discovered the evolution of society as Darwin had discovered the evolution of biological life. Both theories, however, brought the world to the abyss. The struggle for life and the survival of the fittest form the basis for Darwin, for Marx, and for Stalin. Stalin merely put into practice what Marx and Lenin taught. Marx's atheism, dialectical materialism, evolution, and socialism make up the heart of the communist worldview. These are the ideas that were put into practice in the slaughter that occurred during the twentieth century.

Yet, as we enter the twenty-first century, Marxist ideas are still part of the intellectual's quiver. Campus Marxists and postmodernists, for example, continue to propagate atheism, materialism, evolution, socialism, and collectivism. Hardly anything has changed! It is as though we have allowed history to teach us absolutely nothing. Little wonder that Hegel said, "Peoples and government never have learned anything from history, or acted on principles deduced from it."[68] If one is an atheist and an evolutionist, for example, one has immediate access to America's public educational institutions and stands a good chance of winning recognition and awards. If one is a theist and a creationist, one is denied access to such educational institutions and considered a Neanderthal or a trilobite. If one is an atheist, an evolutionist, *and* an advocate of united world government, one has access to all educational institutions and is guaranteed even more awards and foundation grants. Anyone who suggests that U.S. military personnel should not be placed under United Nations control will not be allowed access and will be told he or she is narrow-minded, intolerant, and unloving. The propaganda and name-calling of the Left have not changed for over one hundred years (see Zygmund Dobb's *The Great Deceit: Social Pseudo-Sciences*) and evidently will not change anytime soon.

The theology of Marxism/Leninism/Stalinism is atheistic. Lenin, for example, in his "Socialism and Religion" address insisted that communism is based on the scientific, materialistic view of the world. Therefore, says Lenin, "our propaganda necessarily includes the propaganda of atheism."[69] Elsewhere Lenin said, "Every religious idea, every idea of God, even flirting with the idea of God, is unutterable vileness . . . vileness of the most dangerous kind."[70]

"For Marx and the classical Marxist authors," wrote Hans Küng, "in their personal life, in their culture, in their system and in their practice—atheism was and remained of central importance and essentially connected with their theory of society and history."[71] This led Fyodor Dostoevski (1821–1881) to remark, "The problem of Communism is not an economic problem. The problem of Communism is the problem of atheism."[72]

The philosophy of Marxism/Leninism/Stalinism can be summarized under the term *dialectical materialism*. The heart of the philosophy states two things:

1. Matter is reality.
2. Matter behaves dialectically.[73]

*Dialectical materialism* attempts to explain all of reality—including inorganic matter at the molecular, atomic, and subatomic levels. In the organic world it involves life and (according to materialism) mind or consciousness, and social life in the forms of economics and politics. All of nature reflects, illuminates, and illustrates communist dialectical philosophy. For better or worse, Marxist philosophy is built primarily on the "science" of Darwinian evolution. Matter behaves in an upward progression, from inorganic to organic states, from the organic to human complexities, and from individual to communal human social levels. All respond to certain laws:

1. the unity and struggle of opposites
2. the transformation of quantity into quality
3. the negation of the negation

The dialectical laws manifest a threefold rhythm of equilibrium (thesis), disturbance (antithesis) and reestablishment of equilibrium (synthesis or new thesis). All true Marxists believe that the physical universe acts according to such laws.

The biology of Marxism/Leninism/Stalinism centers on Charles Darwin. According to Marx, "Darwin's *[Origin of Species]* is very important and provides me with the basis in natural science for the class struggle in history."[74] Friedrich Engels (1820–1895) put it like this: "Just as Darwin discovered the law of evolution in organic nature, so Marx discovered the law of evolution in human history."[75] Few doubt that Darwin's theory of evolution and Marx's theory of communism fit hand to glove.

The psychology of Marxism centers on materialistic behaviorism in which people are looked upon as conditioned, evolving animals. Lenin insisted: "Matter is primary nature. Sensation, thought, consciousness, are the highest products of matter organized in a certain way. This is the doctrine of materialism, in general, and Marx and Engels, in particular."[76]

The economics/sociology of Marxism/Leninism/Stalinism can be summarized in a single sentence: Abolish private property.[77] Marx goes on to say in *The Communist Manifesto:* "The communists disdain to conceal their views and aims. They openly declare that their ends can be attained only by the forcible overthrow of all existing social conditions."[78] The three social institutions fit for overthrow are the family, the church, and the state, though few remember that Marx and Engels called for "an openly legalized community of women."[79] Lenin, too, summarized the heart of economics/socialism: "Communist society means that everything— the land, the factories—is owned in common. Communism means working in common."[80] Millions of people were slaughtered to establish a socialist utopia. But then, one can't have an omelet without smashing eggs, and, from a communist point of view, an evolving human animal is no different from an egg.

The law of Marxism/Leninism/Stalinism is simply evolutionary law writ large. There are no legal absolutes because humanity is evolving, and law is evolving with it. There is no eternal lawgiver since, according to their theology, there is no God. Therefore, there are no eternal legal principles. Legal principles that assist in evolutionary, socialistic history are just laws; all others are unjust. Case closed! Marx put it like this: "Law, morality, religion, are to [the proletariat] so many bourgeois prejudices, behind which lurk in ambush just as many bourgeois interests."[81]

The politics of Marxism/Leninism/Stalinism is power. State terror is part and parcel of the "Dictatorship of the Proletariat." Lenin states, "The art of politics lies in correctly gauging the conditions and the moment when the vanguard of the proletariat [the killing machine] can successfully seize power."[82] Engels is likewise brutal: "In reality, however, the State is nothing more than a machine for the oppression of one class by another."[83] The political machinery put together by the disciples of Marx murdered and slaughtered 86 million people. And that figure continues to rise.

The history of Marxism/Leninism/Stalinism consists of one major and a few minor players. The major player is the dialectical nature of matter. All history—all reality—is seen as the outworking of this all-encompassing concept. Dialectical matter is eternal. All else follows from this premise. Dialectical matter determines history. Interestingly, Communists believe in nudging history. Stalin alone was guilty of the persecution, imprisonment, torture and death of 50 million.[84]

Marxist ethics proceed out of Marxist theology, philosophy, biology, economics/sociology, law, politics, and history. It is an ethics that states an absolute: class morality. Whatever advances the proletariat class, by definition, is good. Or put another way, each act is considered ethically good if it assists the flow of history toward a communist end. Killing, raping, stealing, and lying are not outside the boundaries of communist morality. Marxists/Leninists/Stalinists have absolutely no trouble equating the killing of evolving materialistic human beings infected with the concepts of God, transcendent morality, and private property with the killing by a farmer of a materialistic evolving cow afflicted with hoof-and-mouth disease. The killing fields of Cambodia, the Ukraine, Russia, and China were the practical results of class morality. One communist dictator said:

> Our cause is sacred. He whose hand will tremble, who will stop midway, whose knees will shake before he destroys tens and hundreds of enemies, he will lead the revolution into danger. Whoever will spare a few lives of enemies will pay for it with hundreds and thousands of lives of the better sons of our fathers.[85]

If postmodernism is a wayward stepchild of Marxism, intellectuals have learned nothing from this portion of history.[86]

## Secular Humanism

Secular humanism, too, is a worldview. John Dewey in *A Common Faith* said: "Here are all the elements for a religious faith that shall not be confined to sect, class, or race. Such a faith has always been implicitly the common faith of mankind. It remains to make it explicit and militant."[87]

Margaret Sanger represents that aspect of secular humanism that could end up killing more people than Nazism, fascism, and communism combined.

Sanger is the founder of Planned Parenthood, an organization responsible for the death of millions of unborn human beings, and the killings continue with no end in sight. Secular humanists have slaughtered the innocent in order to further the sexual revolution. Sanger, Mary Calderone, and Faye Wattleton have all been accorded the honor "Humanist of the Year" by the American Humanist Association, and all three were heavily involved in promoting the revolution.

If it is possible for one person to change the very foundations of civilization, Sanger rightfully should be known as the founder of modern culture. Today's culture is characterized precisely by the values she and her admirers taught.[88]

H. G. Wells agreed: "Margaret Sanger made currents and circumstances. When the history of our civilization is written, it will be a biological history and Margaret Sanger will be its heroine."[89] As part of the Wantley Circle, a free-love association, Wells (1866–1946) was among those who had a sexual relationship with Sanger.[90]

According to a candid statement published by *Planned Parenthood News* in 1953, the goal of Planned Parenthood is to help "young people obtain sex satisfaction before marriage. By sanctioning sex before marriage, we will prevent fear and guilt."[91] The 1974 Planned Parenthood publication *You've Changed the Combination* states, "There are only two kinds of sex: sex with victims and sex without. Sex with victims is always wrong. Sex without is always right."[92]

Sanger epitomizes the secular humanist worldview. Nothing in her teaching or lifestyle falls outside of secular humanism in theory or practice. Her supporters are all proud of her and her accomplishments.

For example, she founded the publication *The Woman Rebel*, for which the motto was, "No Gods! No Masters!" In her very first edition of *The Woman Rebel* she denounced marriage as "a degenerate institution" and sexual modesty as "obscene prudery."[93] Sanger's personal hero was psychologist Havelock Ellis (1859–1939). Upon reading his seven-volume *Studies in the Psychology of*

*Sex*, she told her husband that she needed to be liberated from the strict bonds of marriage. She ultimately deserted her husband to practice free love in Greenwich Village.

Sanger called for limiting the number of children within the poorer classes of people. She believed the state should license parents to have babies, should forcibly sterilize poor people, and should encourage the more successful to have more children. Her ideal new world order had no crime or poverty caused by the birth of genetically inferior children. She was more successful than Hitler in that she successfully encouraged peaceful methods of racial "purification." She advocated that society's "human weeds" should be paid with money or presents to be sterilized.[94] Yet it was not "human weeds" who were the major players of the twentieth century slaughter. It was Sanger's kind—the well-off and well-educated who prided themselves on being bright enough to determine who lived and who died.

Her relationship with the Nazi worldview involves Ernst Rudin, director of the Nazi Society for Racial Hygiene. In 1933, *Planned Parenthood Review* published Rudin's article, "Eugenic Sterilization: An Urgent Need." Later in 1933, it published an article by Leon Whitney defending the Third Reich's racial cleansing program.[95] In his book *Into the Darkness, Nazi Germany Today*, published in 1940, Sanger colleague Lothrop Stoddard expressed his admiration for the Germans' method of cleaning up their race problems using "scientific and truly humanitarian ways." As George Grant notes, Margaret Sanger was mesmerized by the "scientific" racism of Malthusian eugenics. She followed her lover Ellis, who in turn followed Darwin's cousin Francis Galton, in systematizing and popularizing eugenic thought.

But Sanger's attraction to race was also political. Grant relates, "Virtually all of her Socialist friends, lovers, and comrades, were committed Eugenicists—from the followers of Lenin in Revolutionary Socialism, like H. G. Wells, George Bernard Shaw, and Julius Hammer, to the followers of Hitler in National Socialism, like Ernest Rudin, Leon Whitney, and Harry Laughlin."[96]

While Sanger is representative of secular humanism, John Dewey is its most famous and important voice. Dewey's influence on American education has been dominant since the 1930s. Secular humanism is the only worldview allowed in the public schools. Humanist Charles Francis Potter, in *Humanism: A New Religion*, says: "Education is the most powerful ally of humanism, and every American public school is a school of humanism. What can the theistic Sunday Schools, meeting for an hour once a week, and teaching only a fraction of the children, do to stem the tide of a five-day program of humanistic teaching."[97]

From kindergarten through graduate school, America's students are immersed in the doctrines and dogmas of secular humanism. The U.S. Supreme Court has made sure that only secular humanism is taught in the classroom, in spite of a 1961 Supreme Court ruling that designated secular humanism a religion.[98]

Leftists, socialists, liberals, and humanists slowly but surely captured the social sciences (sociology, anthropology, history, economics, and jurisprudence) and many pulpits. The Veritas Foundation's studies are entitled *The Great Deceit: Social Pseudo-Sciences* and *Keynes at Harvard*. *The Great Deceit* studies Dewey's relationship to the League for Industrial Democracy, the American counterpart to the British Fabian Society.[99] Dewey epitomizes secular humanism since he was an atheist in theology, a naturalist in philosophy, an ethical relativist in morals, an evolutionist in biology, and a socialist in economics.

True secular humanists are frequently quite open about their worldview. They readily admit that they are

### Theological atheists

"Humanism cannot in any fair sense of the word apply to one who still believes in God as the source and creator of the universe."[100]—Paul Kurtz

### Philosophical naturalists

"Naturalistic Humanism . . . is the Humanism that I have supported through the written and spoken word for some forty years."[101]—Corliss Lamont

### Ethical relativists

"No inherent moral or ethical laws exist, nor are there absolute guiding principles for human society. The universe cares nothing for us and we have no ultimate meaning in life."[102]—William Provine

### Biological evolutionists

"Evolution is a fact amply demonstrated by the fossil record and by contemporary molecular biology. Natural selection is a successful theory devised to explain the fact of evolution."[103]—Carl Sagan

### Psychological self-actualizationists

"For myself, though I am very well aware of the incredible

amount of destructive, cruel, malevolent behavior in today's world—from the threats of war to the senseless violence in the streets—I do not find that this evil is inherent in human nature."[104]—Carl Rogers

*Sociological social scientists*

"Marriage, for most people, has outlived its usefulness and is doing more harm than good."[105]—Lawrence Casler

*Judicial positive law upholders*

"No matter how misperceived as natural they may be, rights . . . are the works of human artifice."[106]—Delos B. McKown

*Political globalists*

"It is essential for UNESCO to adopt an evolutionary approach. . . . The general philosophy of UNESCO should, it seems, be a scientific world humanism, global in extent and evolutionary in background. . . . Thus the struggle for existence that underlies natural selection is increasingly replaced by conscious selection, a struggle between ideas and values in consciousness."[107]—Julian Huxley

*Economic socialists*

"A socialized and cooperative economic order must be established to the end that the equitable distribution of the means of life be possible."[108]—*The Humanist Manifesto*

*Historical atheistic evolutionists*

"The laws of biology are the fundamental lessons of history."[109] "War is one of the constants of history and is the ultimate form of natural selection in the human species."[110]—Will and Ariel Durant

## Conclusion

> But sanctify Christ as Lord in your hearts, always being ready to make a defense to everyone who asks you to give an account for the hope that is in you, with gentleness and reverence. (1 Peter 3:15)

Every believer, says Erwin W. Lutzer, in *Hitler's Cross*, should be able to give a rationale for faith, to declare Christ supreme over all other alternatives.[111] The alternative to the twentieth century humanistic worldview is Christ. Lutzer says: "We do not know where all this [the ACLU and liberal left seeking to cleanse the public square of biblical Christianity] will end. What we do know is that we have the high honor of representing Christ in the midst of this ideological mega-shift. Our challenge is to rise to this hour of incredible challenge and opportunity."[112]

Lutzer doesn't think that a two-hour Sunday morning church service will do it. He agrees with Dietrich Bonhoeffer, who said:

> We Lutherans have gathered like eagles around the carcass of cheap grace, and there we have drunk the poison which has killed the life of following Christ. . . . In such a Church the world finds a cheap covering for its sins; no contrition is required, still less any real desire to be delivered from sin. . . . Cheap grace means the justification of sin without the justification of the sinner . . . it is grace without discipleship, grace without the cross, grace without Jesus Christ, living and incarnate.[113]

The question then becomes, Is it worth the effort to live Christ twenty-four hours a day, on one hand, or be a Christian weenie or couch potato, on the other—a spiritual or a carnal Christian? Living Christ twenty-four hours a day is hard. Cheap grace demands the soft life. Living Christ demands discipline, sacrifice, purity, prayer, witness, study, standing alone, and confrontation (Acts 17:16–17). But then the very "being" of life involves theology, philosophy, ethics, biology, and so forth. It demands that we follow Christ in these areas. This is exactly what the Bible teaches.

For example, in theology, Christ is "the fullness of the Godhead" (Col. 2:9). In philosophy, Christ is the "logos" of God (John 1:1–3). In ethics, Christ is "true Light" (John 1:9). In biology, Christ is "Life" (John 1:4). In psychology, Christ is "Savior" of the soul (Luke 1:46–47). In sociology, Christ is "Son" (Luke 1:30–31). In government, Christ is "lawgiver" (Gen. 49:10), "King of Kings, and Lord of Lords" (Rev. 19:16). In economics, Christ is "Owner" of all things (Ps. 50:10–12). In history, Christ is "Alpha and Omega" (Rev. 1:8). None of these areas is secular. All are sacred because they are founded on Jesus Christ. Since Christ is the fountainhead of all wisdom and knowledge (Col. 2:2–3), all areas are open for Christian living and study.[114]

If the twenty-first century is not to be the scene of a slaughter similar to that in the twentieth century, Christians need to listen carefully to Lutzer, who has learned some valuable lessons from his study of the surrender to Nazism of the 1930s German church. "It is time," says Lutzer, "that Christians become leaders in art, education, politics, and law." He could have added theology, philosophy, ethics, the sciences, psychology, sociology, and history.

The mistake of the German church, according to Lutzer was to:

> isolate the spiritual sphere from the political, social, and cultural world. Bonhoeffer was critical of the church when its only interest was self-preservation. We should be characterized by giving, not withholding. Since we share this planet with all of humanity, we must reestablish leadership in all of those areas where Christians often led the way.[115]

# 2

# TECHNOLOGY AND THEOLOGY: REALITY AND HOPE FOR THE THIRD MILLENNIUM

## Timothy J. Demy

As we enter a new century and also a new millennium, it is appropriate that Christians reevaluate and reaffirm their commitment to the Bible; the fundamental doctrines of orthodox Christianity; and the application of those beliefs in a personal, local, and global context. The Christian view of, and response to, technology is only one of the many areas of life that we must examine if we are going to be effective in our Christian witness in the future. D. A. Lyon observes: "The debate over technology will continue to be central to political life in the twenty-first century. Christian contributions to this debate become increasingly important in contexts where secularization has eroded and excluded the sense that there are any real norms to guide technological development."[1]

Though at first glance technology and theology might appear to be mutually exclusive, a very strong connection has been present throughout history. Christian thinkers, at least since the time of Augustine, addressed issues of science and technology, recognizing the importance of understanding the physical world. The argument that Christianity was inherently antiscientific and thwarted the pursuit of science and technology is one that arose in the eighteenth and nineteenth centuries and is inaccurate.[2] For example, in the twelfth century, a treatise entitled *The Various Arts* by a monk, writing under the pseudonym Theophilus, became a standard reference for craftsmen. Thus, the technology employed in building the cathedrals of Europe was also understood to have theological underpinnings.[3] Later, such men as Isaac Newton and Jonathan Edwards would also integrate science, theology, and technology. Christian history is filled with examples of an acceptance of technology and attempts to understand it within a biblical perspective.

With the turning of a page of the calendar, the dawn of a new era of human history begins. The question that remains to be answered in A.D. 2000 and beyond is whether the Christian witness in the future will shine forth, permeating culture, or be eclipsed by the gathering clouds of neopaganism. In a post-Christian culture in the West and a non-Christian culture in the East, the challenge to the Christian testimony is formidable. Perhaps we are not so unlike the Israelites in the wilderness to whom God said: "I have set before you life and death, the blessing and the curse. So choose life in order that you may live, . . . by loving the LORD your God, by obeying His voice, and by holding fast to Him" (Deut. 30:19b–20a). The decisions we make now will affect not only ourselves but also our posterity.

## Technology's Challenge

The greatest technological challenge of the twenty-first century and the third millennium as we await the return of Jesus Christ will not have been the resolution and aftermath of the computer Y2K problem or "millennium bug" (though it is an excellent illustration of the dependency of much of society on technology). Rather, the challenge will be the extent to which technological processes and objects will be molded to God's normative will rather than to pride and selfishness.[4] Will technology and technological activity be pursued within a biblical or secular framework? The extensive presence of technology in Western society is a reality that must be considered within the framework of the Christian worldview. Technology directly or indirectly affects every area of our lives. Whether we consider this good or bad, it is a fact.[5]

One area of concern that Christians should address is the hope that individuals and society as a whole place in technology. For some, technology (with science) has become a false god of hope, the vaunted path toward human perfection. For much of the secularized West, there has been, and continues to be, a pursuit of human perfection and salvation that is technologically based rather than theologically based. Jeremy Rifkin writes of the contemporary ideological quest for a techno-paradise: "In the modern age, the idea of a future technological utopia has served as the guiding vision of industrial society. For more than a century utopian dreamers and men and women of science and letters have looked to a future world where machines would replace human labor, creating a near-workerless society of abundance and leisure."[6]

Rifkin further argues that in the last one hundred years technology has become the "new secular god."[7] How are we, then, to view technology? What are the promises and perils of the future of technology when viewed from a biblical perspective? Is technology a tool, a toy, or a tyrant? The answers we give to these questions can have significant effects on our personal, spiritual, vocational or professional, and social lives.

Numerous helpful volumes have been written on the history of technology, on the phenomenon of technology as a system, and on its nature as a social and political phenomenon, especially with regard to ideas of progress. There have been, however, far fewer investigations of technology from a theological perspective. The majority of the theological writings have not come from the pens of evangelicals; conservative theological critiques have been rare.[8] Yet, within a biblical perspective, technology falls under the responsibilities of the divine mandate to care for and open up the possibilities of the creation. This is because science and technology arises out of an understanding of and interaction with creation. Commonly referred to as the "cultural mandate," we read in Genesis 1:26–28:

> Then God said, "Let Us make man in Our image, according to Our likeness; and let them rule over the fish of the sea and over the birds of the sky and over the cattle and over all the earth, and over every creeping thing that creeps on the earth." And God created man in His own image, in the image of God He created him; male and female He created them. And God blessed them; and God said to them, "Be fruitful and multiply, and fill the earth, and subdue it; and rule over the fish of the sea and over the birds of the sky, and over every living thing that moves on the earth."

With regard to technology and the cultural mandate, Stephen Monsma notes:

> Few systematic reflections on modern technology have been initiated by Christian theologians. Indeed, Christians have often not seriously concerned themselves with either

the negative or the positive consequences of modern scientific-technological development. They have viewed technology either as something that is naturally good or as a development that is neutral in relation to the Christian faith. The point is that even Christians—who in theory accept the cultural mandate as a duty to be carried out in subjection to God's normative will—have in practice often emphasized the theme of progress and cultural development for its own sake, without reference to the divine constraints within which proper and responsible cultural development is sought.

These tendencies—all too often present within Christendom—have been strengthened and reinforced by a secularization movement that has its roots in the Renaissance, the Enlightenment, and modern philosophy. They have come to play a powerful role in modern society in the past two centuries.[9]

The neglect of Christians in addressing technology from a theological perspective has resulted in domination by secularism's view of technology. This view is accepted uncritically by users and developers of technology. As evangelicals view technology and its effects on culture and society, we are left with the dilemma voiced by Carl F. H. Henry more than a quarter of a century ago:

> We live in the twilight of a great civilization, amid the deepening decline of modern culture. Those strange beast-empires of the books of Daniel and Revelation seem already to be stalking and sprawling over the surface of the earth. Only the success of modern science hides us from the dread terminal illness of our increasingly technological civilization. . . . The barbarians are coming; the Lord Jesus Christ is coming. *Christians are here now; do they know whether they are coming or going?*[10]

What is our response to this question, and in what areas of technology should Christians exert major efforts? The barbarians may indeed be coming, but they are also coming in full technological force (literally as well as figuratively).[11] Before we can answer these questions, we should briefly view the different perspectives regarding technology.

## *The Good, the Bad, the Ugly*

Though we think of technology as machines or computers, it also refers to systems and processes. The word *technology* is derived from the Greek roots *techno* (art, skill, or craft) and *logos* (word, study). When we think of technology today, we think not only of tools but also of crafts or techniques for doing something. Thus, technology may be defined as "the application of organized knowledge to practical tasks by ordered systems of people and machines."[12]

Within the history and philosophy of technology there have been three major views—*technology as liberator, technology as threat*, and *technology as instrument of power*. Three comments from representatives of these views illustrate the positions respectively:

> Technology, the source of the problem, will once again prove to contain within itself the germs of a solution compatible with the betterment of man's lot and dignity.[13]

> Our enslavement to the machine has never been more complete.[14]

> What we call Man's power over Nature turns out to be a power exercised by  some men over other men with Nature as its instrument.[15]

Most Christian thinkers have supported the second and third perspectives—technology as a threat or as an instrument of power. Though aspects of the technology-as-threat perspective are appealing, the third viewpoint is accepted in this essay.

### Technology as Liberator

The arguments of those who see technology as a liberator are fourfold:

1. Technology provides higher living standards and quality of life.
2. Technology provides opportunity for choice.
3. Technology provides more leisure.
4. Technology provides improved communication.[16]

Critics of the view reply that these four benefits come at a great cost to individuals and society. This cost entails

- environmental liabilities and human risks;
- alienation from nature and the created order;

- concentration of economic and political power in the hands of the few rather than the many;
- large-scale technologies that are capital intensive and vulnerable to error, accident, or sabotage;
- creation of a society with a very high dependence on experts;
- a linear view of the science-technology-society relationship in which technology is normally understood to have a one-way impact on society.[17]

While aspects of the technology-as-liberator view are attractive at first sight, as a philosophical framework for understanding technology this view is inadequate and underestimates the broken nature of humanity due to sin. Technological optimism does not match well with theological reality.

**Technology as Threat**

At the opposite end of the spectrum are those who view technology essentially as a threat. Adherents of this view are such notable and diverse religious representatives as Jacques Ellul, Paul Tillich, Martin Buber, and the Amish. Technological pessimists, who see technology primarily as a threat to contemporary society and individuals, suggest five major human costs of technology:

1. Technology creates uniformity in a society at the expense of individuality.
2. Technology creates narrow criteria for efficiency, minimizing meaningful work roles.
3. Technology promotes impersonality and manipulates people.
4. Technology creates its own social momentum that tends to make technology itself uncontrollable.
5. Technology contributes to the impoverishment of human relationships, the loss of community, and alienation in the workplace.[18]

Three replies have been offered against the technological pessimists:

1. The great variations among technologies defy generalized condemnation.
2. A negative view of technology neglects possible avenues for the redirection of technology.
3. Technology, if properly used, can serve human values.[19]

Aspects of this view also have merit. However, as an overall philosophy of technology, it does not adequately address all of the concerns and issues.

### Technology as Instrument of Power

The third view of technology, technology as an instrument of power, "holds that technology is neither inherently good nor inherently evil but is an ambiguous instrument of power whose consequences depend on its social context."[20] This is not to say that technology is neutral even though it often appears to be so. Because there is a historical context for its development and ethical decisions were made regarding it, technology is not neutral. Ian Barbour illustrates this:

> A knife can be used for surgery or for murder. An isotope separator can enrich uranium for peaceful nuclear reactors or for aggression with nuclear weapons. But historical analysis suggests that most technologies are already molded by particular interests and institutional goals. Technologies are social constructions, and they are seldom neutral because particular purposes are already built into their design. Alternative purposes would lead to alternative designs. Yet most designs still allow some choice as to how they are deployed.[21]

Because technology is not developed in a social and ethical vacuum, nor used in one, it is not neutral for either the creator or the consumer. Ethical decisions are always included in the development of new technologies, either directly or indirectly. Research and development of one technology means that those same resources will not be used for other areas. Choices always entail consequences. Proponents of this third view include Barbour, Monsma, Egbert Schuurman, Roger Shinn, C. S. Lewis, and H. Richard Niebuhr. Barbour writes of the relationship of this position to Christianity:

> This third position seems to me more consistent with the biblical outlook than either of the alternatives. Preoccupation with technology does become a form of idolatry, a denial of the sovereignty of God, and a threat to distinctively human existence. But technology directed to genuine human needs is a legitimate expression of human kind's creative capacities and an essential contribution to its welfare.[22]

Technology influences human life but is also a part of the social and cultural system. It is therefore an instrument of power that serves the purposes of those who control it and use it—either for good or for evil.

Among the most significant areas of life affected by technology are food, health, work, and personal fulfillment. In each of these areas there is potential for great good and great abuse. Each of these also relates significantly to the broader issues of justice, freedom, rights, and democracy.[23] Technology is therefore inextricably linked to the realm of economics and politics as well as theology. Without a biblical perspective, confusion, chaos, and manipulation will soon prevail in any of these areas.

## A Biblical Perspective

Within a Christian worldview, our perspective of technology must be seen in the context of the cultural mandate. David Gill notes that "any theological critique of technology must return to the biblical sources. There we find that technology is an expression of divinely created human creativity and imagination, of doing and making good and helpful life-enhancing things."[24] As a means of assisting in human endeavors, technology, if used within its purposes and limits, is good. As an example of this, we find in Deuteronomy 22:8 the requirement to incorporate safety features in building design. As a means of fulfilling the cultural mandate, technology is a good thing, but, like everything else, it is also affected by the intrusion of sin into the world. The potential for the misdirection of technology is always present. As a result of the Fall, some technology came to be used for destructive purposes, especially in warfare, and there arose also a dependence upon technology. Lyon writes:

> Not only are tools used destructively as weapons, but an element of transferred trust is also present, later to be denounced by prophetic woes on those who *rely on* their chariots and spears (Isa. 31:1–3). The story of the tower of Babel (Gen. 11:1–9) represents a particularly low point in technological history, where the whole project is both breathtaking in conception and idolatrous in intention.[25]

Just as technology was affected by the Fall, so also will it be affected by the final redemption of creation in the millennial kingdom (Rom. 8:22). It is at this time that the effects of the Fall will be reversed. Technology that has been used for destructive purposes will be transformed for socially constructive uses. It will be at this time that "they will hammer their swords into plowshares and their spears into pruning hooks; nation will not lift up sword against nation, and never again will they train for war" (Mic. 4:3). As an instrument of power, technology can be used for good or evil by fallen humanity. "The biblical viewpoint, significantly, stresses the salience of all three features—creation, broken covenant and redemption—in interpreting technological activity."[26]

A biblical perspective of technology is far different from a secular perspective in which there is a drive for human autonomy and mastery of the environment apart from God and the will of God. This latter perspective might best be called *technicism*, not technology. Such a view "reduces all things to the technological; it sees technology as the solution to all human problems and needs. Technology is a savior, the means to make progress and gain mastery over modern, secularized cultural desires."[27] Similarly, Lyon defines *technicism* as "the belief in human autonomy and power, manifest in technological development."[28] Within technicism, there is an assumption of human sovereignty and human progress. In technicism, technology becomes its own reason for existing. In essence, technicism says that if something can be done, it should be done. No questions should be asked, and it is understood that "You can't stop progress!" Technicism believes that the fate of men and women rests in their own hands and that progress is not only possible but also inevitable in every area of existence. With the assistance of technology, a techno-paradise, if not perfection is just over the horizon.[29] Such a perspective is antithetical to a biblical perspective, yet it is the prevailing philosophy of technology in the world. Technicism becomes a theological problem that is manifested in the economic, political, and social realms of daily life in the industrialized world. Monsma writes:

> Because society as a whole has adopted the faith of technicism, government is unable to play an effective role in justly directing technological structures. The heart of the problem turns out to be religious. The command to love God above all and one's neighbor as oneself needs to be followed. Not that technology and its fruits are always evil. In fact, they are often good. What is needed is a means to properly evaluate and judge technologies, and that comes from following biblically based normative principles. Such principles need to replace technicism as humankind's guiding principles.[30]

A biblical perspective of technology is soundly at odds with our contemporary culture and is unlikely to ever become the prevailing perspective. Yet we still have the obligation to practice and preach the principles of such a view. To the extent that we are competent and have the opportunity to influence our society, we must do so. Monsma is correct when he states:

> The cadence of our culture is set by the beat of the technological drum. In and of itself, this basic fact should be cause for neither great rejoicing nor great alarm. The crucial question is, if this is so, who or what is determining the beat? . . . In modern society this beat is largely determined by a drive for power, for human mastery apart from the will of God. Humankind has revolted against its Maker, has declared its independence from him and his will, and all too often drives ruthlessly for a salvation of material prosperity brought about by technological prowess.[31]

As we look toward a biblical perspective of technology, there are two extremes we must avoid. The first is trying to deduce a complete system of social knowledge and societal structure from Christian principles—the facts are too diverse, society too complex, and the human mind too limited. This does not mean however, that there are no Christian principles of social action and social order. A second extreme is complete withdrawal from society and culture and a view that all perspectives and judgments are personal, subjective, and private.[32]

### Characteristics of Technology

What are the characteristics and principles that we might look for in a biblically based view of technological activity? There are three characteristics of Christian normative principles for technological activities that should be considered as a foundation.[33] First, an adequate Christian normative character must be broad in its scope. Since everything in a theistic universe is value-laden, there is no neutrality and there are many points of contact between technology and other aspects of life. "Indeed, opposing the idea that technology is neutral implies that technology neither begins nor proceeds in a value-free manner, nor are its effects on society neutral."[34] Because it affects so many areas of life, we cannot look at technology in isolation. Technological activity must be firmly rooted in the love of God and others (Matt. 22:37–39). The overarching principle or umbrella for technological activity is love: love of God above all and love of one's neighbor as oneself.

Second, Christian normative characteristics for technological activities must differentiate between God and humans and between humans and other aspects of creation. There is diversity within the creation, and Christian normative principles for technology must recognize this and make necessary distinctions within creation.[35] The principle of love that is to be expressed is done so in varying ways within the spheres of human existence. For example, love of neighbor is different from love of family. Because there are so many facets to our lives and because technology affects all of these facets, we must make distinctions regarding the created diversity of human existence. Third, and finally, having recognized diversity within creation, Christian normative principles for technology must "integrate the diversity found in society so that there is no conflict among its facets."[36] Each of the three characteristics for doing technology, however, comes under the umbrella or mandate of love.

Because technological activity is a form of cultural activity, it is a way of partially fulfilling the cultural mandate and reflecting the commandment of love. Our pursuit of technology is, first, a form of service to God, then care and concern for other human beings, and finally, care and cultivation of the natural creation. "We are called to do technology in such a way that the creativity and joy for which God created men and women can exist in abundance, the riches of the physical world can be uncovered and utilized, and the plant and animal worlds can be perceived and used for what they are and for what God intends them to be."[37] A biblically based perspective such as this means that in technological activity, humans are to show respect for the various entities of creation and use them according to divine intent. Thus, appropriate use or development of a resource or technological process will require evaluation and discernment that extends beyond economic feasibility or profitability. Additionally, technological activity from a biblical perspective means that such activity reflects a love of God and neighbor by expanding rather than limiting opportunities for human freedom and action. Technology should assist others as well as us to fulfill responsibilities before God.[38]

## Principles for Technology

What are the principles that should guide us in technological activity? As we attempt to construct a biblical philosophy of technology that incorporates love, recognition of created diversity, and integration of diversity, there are several principles that should guide technological endeavors. All of the principles found on this list are present in varying degrees in the writings of religious and secular philosophies of technology. A distinctively biblical perspective includes some, excludes others, and values each differently. These principles are developed at length by Monsma et al., in *Responsible Technology: A Christian Perspective*. While other principles might be added and some combined, a biblical perspective should include, in some manner, seven principles:

1. *Cultural appropriateness*: Technologies that erode or destroy cultural activities reflecting biblical values should not be used. This means that there must be careful thought and discussion in public and private forums before pursing the research and development of technology.
2. *Communication and openness of information*: The development and use of technology involves language and numbers. Therefore, if it is going to be developed and used responsibly, there must be accurate information about it.
3. *Stewardship*: Technological development and use of human and natural resources must be done from an attitude of respect rather than from reckless exploitation. Stewardship recognizes that there is more at stake than economics.
4. *Delightful harmony*: Technological development and activity should relate to humans and the rest of creation in manners that aesthetically satisfy and functionally promote right relationships.
5. *Justice*: All activity pertaining to technology must give people and creation that which is rightfully due them, including proper respect.
6. *Caring*: In conjunction with stewardship and justice, there must be the moral aspect of care regarding the use and results of technology. Technology should serve and safeguard that which is entrusted to us.
7. *Trust*: The product or activity must be dependable and safe enough that it earns trust. Also, there must be trust or faith in God so that technology and activity does not become an altar at which to worship human autonomy.[39]

Each of these principles must be pursued simultaneously, and each is an aspect of the single norm of love. We are not at liberty to choose which principles we will apply and which we will ignore. Though the "final product" of their application will vary, depending upon circumstances, they must all be applied in every circumstance.

Application of the principles presents an enormous challenge, but it is necessary if we are to uphold a Christian worldview. A biblical perspective of technology does not say that technology is good or bad. Rather, it argues that technology is an instrument of power that sometimes brings good and sometimes brings evil. A biblical perspective strives to replace the perspective of technicism and to articulate normative principles for judging technological activities and endeavors.

Because technology affects so many areas of human existence, it necessarily touches on many areas of theology. Theology and technology intersect at many points. Biblical perspectives regarding humanity intersect with contemporary bioethics and biotechnology, environmental concerns, and issues of energy and agriculture. The doctrine of sin intersects with issues of technology and privacy, technology and economics, technology and justice, technology and government, and technology and warfare. The doctrine of soteriology and evangelism intersects with communications and transportation. The doctrines of the church and spiritual life touch on the broad realm of cultural engagement, worship, idolatry, and values. Doctrines of the person and work of Christ affect how we view technology and the redemption of creation. The doctrine of eschatology relates to technological concerns of power, progress, and peace. The doctrine of creation is important to technology and humanity and to technology and the environment.

Directly or indirectly, technology and theology correspond at every turn. Yet there are also vast differences, primarily between technicism and a biblical perspective. In technicism, we find both worship and abuse of technology. Technicism, in effect, places the future in the human hand, rather than God's hand. It holds that failure to resolve global dilemmas are failures of the human intellect rather than of the human heart.

"Technicism is the attempt to locate technical solutions to nontechnical problems," observes Robert Wauzzinski, who stresses that such tragedies as the radioactivity released at Chernobyl or the loss of life in the Challenger explosion can be avoided only when *humility* reduces the scope of technology. They are not stopped by *adding* new systems. Because optimists find their remedies for all of life's problems in technology, they saturate culture with technical objects.[40] Technicism produces an uncritical and undiscerning optimism for both the short-term and the long-term future of humanity. Such optimism is at odds with the biblical perspective. The arrogance of science and technology has rendered God and theology irrelevant for many in contemporary society.

Though not all who work in these fields share this perspective, it is the prevailing viewpoint.[41] Christian cultural critic Craig M. Gay writes of the secular perspective:

> From a scientific and theological point of view, God's existence is largely irrelevant. He has been left to inhabit only that space defined by our ever-diminishing scientific ignorance, and so has become the doubtful "god-of-the-gaps." And what little need we may still have for this god-of-the-gaps should, at some point in our technological future, diminish practically to the vanishing point.[42]

Science and technology have influenced the spiritual life as well as the material life:

> Science and technology have substantially reinforced the *plausibility* of practical atheism in modern society and culture. They have made it easier for us to go about our daily business and even to live our entire lives without giving God much thought. . . . This is largely because science and technology define the world in such a way as to render God *practically* irrelevant. Science and technology also encourage us to become so preoccupied with our own knowing and making that we tend to forget that we are ourselves creatures within a larger Creation.[43]

Though the prevailing winds of society and culture are blowing away from God and theology, there remains, as always, individual responsibility and accountability before God.

Technology and science will certainly enhance life for much of the world's population in the future. Christians must not turn their backs on these endeavors. Rather, we must support responsible technology based on a Christian worldview and biblical principles. Technology can be a great asset in the proclamation of the redeeming work of Christ. Technology inevitably changes lives and lifestyles, but it does not change the gospel of Jesus Christ, doctrines of orthodoxy, or other Christian commitments.

## *Areas of Concern*

In the future, several areas of technological endeavor will have enormous effects within industrialized societies: (1) biotechnology and bioethics; (2) communications and computers; (3) wealth, energy, and environmental concerns; and (4) warfare. Concerns related to the biomolecular revolution and the computer revolution will be briefly noted to illustrate the concerns found in many areas of inquiry.

## Biotechnology and Bioethics

Science and technology have brought enormous medical advances and benefits to humanity. The ability to diagnose, prevent, and treat many medical conditions has enriched and saved millions of lives. There have been great leaps in medical care, due in part to technology. No reasonable individual would suggest abandoning such progress. Yet advances in medicine and technology do raise new ethical issues that need to be continually refined and answered.

Many issues previously were not major concerns, for example end-of-life decisions, fetal-tissue research, genetic engineering, genetic testing, gene therapy, biopatents, cloning, and reproductive technology. In each of these areas, there are many ethical decisions. These can be complex problems without simple solutions—ethically or medically. But decisions must be made, with or without Christian responses. It is critical that Christians understand the issues and influence the decision-making process at every level.[44]

New abilities create new questions. Questions of "Can we?" must always be followed by "Should we?" Mathematician and minister John Polkinghorne, a member of the Human Genetics Advisory Commission in the United Kingdom, in an extended but insightful passage, writes:

> Not everything that can be done should be done. The technological imperative, encouraging the continuing pioneering of new techniques, must be tempered by the moral imperative, requiring that such techniques should be achieved by ethically acceptable means and employed for ethically acceptable ends. The search for wise decisions must involve the relevant scientific experts (for only they have the access to the knowledge on which the assessments of possibility and consequences can be based), but it cannot be delegated to them alone (for they possess no necessarily unique insight beyond the topic of their professional expertise). There must be other parties in the debate, which centers on the nature of the respect and restraint due to human life and to human moral dignity. Here theology, with its insight that the

good and perfect will of God the Creator is the true origin of all value, has an important contribution to make. Theology will not seek to stifle advances that could benefit humankind in acceptable ways, but it will insist that the means by which these desirable ends are achieved must themselves be of ethical integrity.[45]

With regard to the debates over genetic engineering and human cloning, it is essential that Christians be informed and responsible, rather than ignorant and reactionary. Theologian R. Albert Mohler Jr., correctly observes: "Christians should engage in this debate on biblical terms and contend for the sanctity of all created life as well as for the distinction between the creature and the Creator. All technologies, including modern genetics, must be evaluated in terms of the biblical revelation and the totality of the Christian worldview."[46] Christians cannot afford to ignore the social debates and concerns of the age. Our hope is indeed, in the person, work, and return of Jesus Christ. However, we have responsibilities in the present world, regardless of the transitory nature of our presence.

While we await the realization of the kingdom of God, there is another world coming upon us in which we may bear witness of the gospel of Jesus Christ. It is not a world that is ushered in by God; it is by humans. It is not in the distant future; it is tomorrow. Mohler warns that:

> the troubling tangle of ethical issues involved in genetic technologies represents an urgent challenge to the Christian church as the people of truth. The new technologies cannot be naively dismissed or blissfully embraced. This generation of Christians must regain the disciplines of moral discernment and cultural engagement. The Brave New World is upon us.[47]

It is indeed a new world, and Christians cannot afford to ignore the signs of the times. There is too much at stake.

Over a half century ago, in the aftermath of World War II and the war crimes tribunal at Nuremberg, Dr. Leo Alexander, a psychiatrist who worked with the Office of the Chief of Counsel for War Crime at Nuremberg, published a landmark paper entitled "Medical Science under Dictatorship."[48] In this paper, he reviewed the medical practices and propaganda employed by the Nazis as they suspended ethical principles and pursued aberrant procedures and gruesome techniques under the guise of medical science. What concerned him was the relative ease with which such research and practices were initiated. What is so troubling to many observers today is that procedures and perspectives that fifty years ago brought judgment as war crimes, are today widely accepted. They are both legal and topics of general discussion.

## Communications and Computers

The computer revolution of the last two decades has radically changed the world and the way many of its inhabitants live. Rifkin observes, "Throughout the world there is a sense of momentous change taking place—change so vast in scale that we are barely able to fathom its ultimate impact. Life as we know it is being altered in fundamental ways."[49] The amount of information and kinds of information we can communicate globally is phenomenal. Computers have touched every area of life. We now have a truly global economy, and global concerns rapidly become personal concerns. Staggering amounts of information are available to anyone with a phone line and a personal computer.

But information is also power. For all the good things that we receive because of computers, there should also be concerns of privacy and power. The ability that we now have to gather vast amounts of information leads to the question of what information should become public and what should remain private. How much should other people, institutions, or governments be allowed to know about your life? What are the boundaries, and who will establish them?

The amount of information that someone has about you is a factor in determining how much influence or control there will be over you. Privacy is the door through which power must pass in order to gain access to information about us. Once that door is opened, we become vulnerable to manipulation and control.[50] A decade ago, Alvin Toffler wrote that the control of knowledge "is the crux of tomorrow's worldwide struggle for power in every human institution."[51] Nothing in the realm of communications and computers has negated his prediction.

We must remember that not all problems have technological answers. Nor do all people benefit from current technology. We must never confuse the technology of the industrialized countries with the living standards of the emerging countries. More than half the world's population still lives more than a two-day walk from a telephone. Over 65 percent of the world's households do not have telephones.[52] Medical resources and capacities at the Mayo Clinic in Minnesota are vastly different from those of a missionary clinic in Mogadishu, Somalia. In the former, medical breakthroughs

are anticipated and experienced routinely; in the latter, the alloca-
tion of scarce resources means that patients will die for lack of
medication that we can buy over the counter at the local pharmacy.

## Technology and Prophecy

For Christians who firmly believe the Bible and its prophetic
teachings, there are often questions raised about technology and
the horrors that may be perpetrated with it. Certainly there is cause
for concern about the potential uses of some technologies. However, one thing we must not do is rush to condemn all technological advances and practices because of our views of the future. It is
wrong to think that because something may or will be used for evil
in the future, we should therefore avoid it or resolutely reject it in
the present. It is much more important that we identify, understand, and nurture the attributes of Christian maturity than it is
that we attempt to identify the mark of the Beast (Rev. 13:11–18).
What is written on the heart is more important than what will be
written on the head. Ultimately, people will lead to Armageddon,
not armor. Our interpretation of the events of Revelation must not
dissuade us from responsibly pursuing or using technology.[53]

An understanding of the Bible and its worldview does not forbid
the use of technology. But we must be aware of technology's potential. The technology that we use today is always subject to be
used for evil tomorrow: that which is intended for good is always
in danger of being abused and corrupted by the heart. The problem
of evil is not an issue of technology but of theology.

## Between Eden and Babel

We have often heard the expression "between a rock and a hard
place" used to express the dilemmas that we sometimes face because of the circumstances in which we find ourselves. Though we
might use such an expression to describe the technological quan-
daries of the present age, there is more accurate imagery from the
pages of Scripture.

Two images stand out in relation to Christian ethics and technological power—Eden and Babel.[54] In Eden there was dominion over
the garden and the responsibility to maintain it (Gen. 1:26; 2:15).
There were also limits to that dominion (Job 39–41; Amos 5:8). There
was a responsibility to maintain the creation, and there were
boundaries to human control. In Babel we find the second image
(Genesis 11). In this image, we see ambition, arrogance, the quest
for power, and the desire to be like God. In this instance, technological endeavor and pride resulted in chaos with enduring effects.

Though we cannot replicate the grandeur of the garden, we can easily succumb to the boastful building of Babel.

In Genesis 12, the chapter following the account of the tower at Babel, we find other construction projects. After the calling of Abraham, two altars were constructed to commemorate the blessing received from God (Gen. 12:7–8). At Babel, technology was used to serve human desires and plans. In Eden, at Shechem, and between Bethel and Ai, technology was used to serve God. We have the same option in our day; we can either serve God or self. David Gill writes of this contrast:

> As Christians we know we cannot go back to Eden. We must go forward either to Babylon, where Babel's project is fulfilled, or to the New Jerusalem, where Abraham's project is fulfilled. The afterlife is depicted in the form of a city, not a new garden, into which the nations bring their glory. We must pray and work that something of our own generation's technology might be worthy of a place in that city of God.[55]

The choices we make in life carry vast consequences, and we must make them carefully and prayerfully.

Technology is carrying us to new frontiers in many areas of life. We therefore need to continually critique our culture and our society from a biblical perspective. Not all that is labeled "progress" is morally and ethically acceptable. Christians categorically reject some technologies because they violate biblical principles. Individual Christians can decide not to use others because to do so would violate conscience, even though it is in an area of Christian liberty. We must know what we believe, why we believe it, and attempt to understand the ramifications of those beliefs.

## Prophetic Living Today

As one watches the news, reads the papers, and considers one's own life, one frequently can wonder whether the world is experiencing the dawn of a new and glorious age or the eve of destruction. The Bible has the answer and will serve as our guide if we permit it to do so. It will also serve as our critic in all of life's endeavors—technological or otherwise. Carl Henry writes: "The Bible is still the most incisive critic of our age. It confronts our broken love of God, our dull sense of justice, our shameful moral nakedness, our waning sense of ethical duty, our badly numbed consciences, our clutching anxieties, the ghastly horrors and brutal violence of this era."[56] We must strive daily to understand the foundation of our beliefs and our actions.

Public and private actions and personal values have consequences. There is truly "a world of difference" between a Christian and a non-Christian worldview. The purpose and role of technology is part of that worldview. We must ask not only what new technologies will be but also how they will be used. Carl Mitchum, who has written extensively on philosophy and technology, notes:

> We do not live in order to make and use technologies; we make and use technologies in order to live—that is, to live one way rather than another. Given our medical, industrial, and computer technologies, we can seek to assess their benefits and risks and to submit them to the principles of justice, or leave them in the hands of amoral market forces. . . . No matter how we decide to treat the environment, no matter what we decide to do with our computers, it will have an ethical, not just a technical, impact on our lives.[57]

Though most of us will not create technology, we all will consume technology. Responsibility is therefore not an option; it is incumbent upon us as human beings. Writing to all citizens of democratic societies, Barbour states: "In sum, citizen participation in a technological society is a difficult but not impossible task. Even a relatively small number of informed and active citizens can contribute to greater public awareness and can enhance the accountability of legislators and officials. Public debate may delay decisions, but it is the lifeblood of democracy."[58]

What is true for all citizens, in this instance, is even more a mandate for Christians, who should have a national, global, and heavenly perspective.

If we are going to speak the truth to a technological age, we must be prepared to warn against the idolatry of technicism, remind our materialistic and technological culture that Jesus Christ offers liberation from the status quo, and stand willing to condemn the excesses and evils that technology may produce.[59] Writing of the Christian responsibility to confront secular society in one realm of technological activity, Monsma observed that "Christians will not always agree on which public policies best sort out the permissible from the impermissible. But the uncertainties of gray issues do not preclude a condemnation of those immoral genetic experiments that wantonly disregard the sacredness of personhood."[60]

This is true in other areas of technology as well. To the extent that we have the ability and opportunity, we should set forth technological advances that we believe should be developed. Gay reminds us: "We do not need to renounce human creativity, therefore; nor do we need to completely forgo technological making; rather, we need only insist that this creative activity be informed by the love of Christ, by the love of neighbor, and by the love of the world for the sake of both."[61] We must also be careful to avoid idle speculation over far-fetched ideas. However, if we apply principles rather than looking at projections that may or may not come to pass, we will be on much firmer ground and retain the credibility of the biblical worldview.

The hope of the future rests firmly in the person and work of Jesus Christ and in His return. The present and future ramifications of technology are extremely important for us to understand. However, the greater challenge is that of the reality of a present Christless society. Though the ethical concerns of technology's influence on our culture are significant, their importance fades in the light of the urgency of the gospel of Jesus Christ.

## It's Time to Pray and Act

The mechanical clock had its origin in the Benedictine monasteries of the late Middle Ages. Daniel Boorstin finds that both interesting and significant: "The first steps toward the mechanical measurement of time, the beginnings of the modern clock in Europe, came not from farmers or shepherds, nor from merchants or craftsmen, but from religious persons anxious to perform promptly and regularly their duties to God. Monks needed to know the times for their appointed prayers."[62] Because they prayed at intervals during the night as well as the day, monks needed to have an instrument that could be heard in the darkness as well as in the light. Thus, the first mechanical clocks were designed not to *show* the time but to *sound* it.

Though it was originally designed to assist the monks in regulating their prayer lives, the clock was soon used by those outside the monastery walls for their own purposes. Originally designed to call men and women to prayer in adoration of God, it soon called men and women to work in adoration of wealth. The original desire for the technology that led to the mechanical clock was not wrong, nor was the design or the initial usage. There was even benefit and positive application by the larger society as the technology spread. What was faulty were those human hearts that used it solely for the glory of gold.

Therein is the challenge for us today as we seek to wisely use technology and develop the resources that God has entrusted to us. As we do so, may we continually remember that our ultimate hope is not in this life but in the one to come. "For we know that if the earthly tent which is our house is torn down, we have a building from God, a house not made with hands, eternal in the heavens" (2 Cor. 5:1).

# 3

# GROWING MYSTICISM VERSUS TRUE BIBLICAL SPIRITUALITY

## Thomas Ice

Sometime in the 1980s, American culture shifted from "What do you think about . . . ?" to "How do you feel about . . . ?" Since then, the evangelical church has been drifting right along with the secular tide. This transformation of the culture is usually known as the shift from modernism to postmodernism. The postmodern mentality is having a huge impact upon American evangelicalism, especially in the areas of Christian living and spirituality. Spirituality within American evangelicalism has gone from a focus upon character development to metaphysical mysticism.

### *The Air We Breath*

First John 4:15 commands believers "not to love the world nor the things in the world." John is warning against "the world," which has to do with the non-Christian mentality that dominates humanity at a given time, while "the things in the world" speaks of the physical universe and man-made items.

The biblical concept of worldliness has more to do with a way of thinking, a mind-set, or worldview, than with particular actions. From generation to generation, from decade to decade, the dominant worldly ideas change. Satan is constantly working behind the scenes to influence the attitudes and ideas that in turn influence each generation. In one generation, worldliness may involve an "anything goes" morality; in another, it may be expressed through rigid morality. Worldliness is best understood as a philosophy of life or a way of thinking that stirs up the flesh to indulge in specific sins such as sexual immorality, drunkenness, or gossip. Worldliness often provides us with a rationale for sin. Thus, worldliness is often associated with false teachings that blind people to the truth and lead them away from God (2 Cor. 4:4).

*Worldliness* is "world-likeness, or resembling the world." In the New Testament, the word *world*, from which we derive our English word *worldly*, or *worldliness*, is translated from the Greek noun *kosmos*, from which we get our English word *cosmetics*. *Kosmos* was used to signify the orderly arrangement of individual parts into an integrated whole, as of the orderly arrangement of soldiers in battle formation.

Thus, in Greek thought, the concept of beauty and order were linked. So *kosmos* often expresses the idea of beautiful arrangement or adornment or decoration. This word, which the Holy Spirit has chosen, is appropriate. Satan loves to decorate his ideas with the most beautiful external attire. We should understand the words *world*, *worldly*, and *worldliness* as the external arrangement of nonbiblical thinking. Worldliness, then, is an organized and attractive system of ideas, concepts, attitudes, and methods that Satan uses to compete with God's view of life and how people should live on planet earth. Satan is the controller of this system of thinking. Whenever we think like the world, we are thinking just like Satan wants us to think. Lewis Sperry Chafer, an outstanding Bible teacher of a previous generation, has described the world system in the following way:

> The *cosmos* is a vast order or system that Satan has promoted, which conforms to his ideals, aims, and methods. It is civilization now functioning apart from God—a civilization in which none of its promoters really expect God to share, who assign to God no consideration in respect to their projects. This system embraces its godless governments, conflicts, armaments, jealousies, its education, culture, religions of morality, and pride. It is that sphere in which man lives. It is what he sees, what he employs. To the uncounted multitude it is all they ever know so long as they live on this earth. It is properly styled *the satanic system*, which phrase is in many instances a justified interpretation of the so-meaningful word, *cosmos*. It is literally a *cosmos diabolicus*.[1]

Worldliness is often presented as something that is beautiful, desirable, enlightening, and, as Eve thought after agreeing with

Satan's temptation, "a delight to the eyes, and . . . desirable to make one wise" (Gen. 3:6). As Genesis 3:6 indicates, Eve was ready, willing, and able to sin when she looked at things from Satan's point of view rather than from God's. Worldliness is Satan's window dressing that presents evil in a way that makes it seem like the good, right, and proper thing to do. When a person is not actively trusting God's Word for direction, it is very easy to be deceived into adopting worldly thinking. In fact, all one has to do to become worldly is to do nothing. The mentality is not only taught; it is more often caught. It is "in the air we breath," and, if not filtered out by God's Word, it provides the mentality through which we think—even about Christianity. Believers can produce a worldly form of Christianity. Such forms are ubiquitous through church history.

## From Rationalism to Mysticism

The Lord told Israel in Deuteronomy 4:2, "You shall not add to the word which I am commanding you, nor take away from it, that you may keep the commandments of the LORD your God which I command you." This passage lays out three responses to God's Word: (1) adding to the Word; (2) taking away from the Word; or (3) keeping or obeying God's Word. This passage makes it clear that God's Word is to be obeyed, not criticized by adding to or taking away, as still goes on today.

It can be noted from this passage that Israel could either obey or disobey God's commandments. Within the realm of unbelief, there are two options, adding to the Word or taking away from the Word. I believe that the liberal takes away from God's Word through epistemological rationalism where an individual sits above God's Word, so to speak, to determine if God has really spoken. This is the tactic of pre-World War II modernism, which said that the Bible is not really the inspired Word of God because we have applied reason and concluded that it is not.

The logical outgrowth of modernism's rationalism is the current postmodern mysticism that often desires to add human thought to God's Word. There have been, they insist, new revelations. There seems to be a progression in the usual attack on God's Word:

1. *Rationalism*, the exaltation of reason above revelation as the grid for evaluating reality, begins the assault.
2. *Skepticism*, wherein everything is questioned, follows.
3. *Mysticism* arises, based on subjective feelings rather than objective truth. In such an epistemology, individuals can and

do come to believe almost anything. Without a doubt, evangelicalism is currently in the midst of what is called postmodern mysticism.

Biblical Christianity should follow neither rationalism nor mysticism as its basis for authority. Instead, it starts with revelation—God's Word—as a basis for truth. God's Word is above any human thought or feeling, "since He [God] could swear by no one greater, He swore by Himself" (Heb. 6:13b). Thus, the ultimate authority as a basis for truth is God's revealed Word, which we know as the Bible. Psalm 36:9 says, "For with Thee is the foundation of life; in Thy light we see light." Psalm 119:130 declares, "The unfolding of Thy words gives light; it gives understanding to the simple." The Bible tells us that we come to know truth by God's gracious revelation of Himself. We can either respond to His Word by submitting in dependence to it and thinking God's own thoughts or by rebelling against His light and thinking our own thoughts.

There may be two ways to *search* for truth, but there is only one way to *find* truth and that is by taking God's word for it. In fact, since "the sum of Thy word is truth" (Ps. 119:160), to look for truth in any other place than in God's Word is to guarantee that you will not find it. This point is driven home by Christ in His comments about the two ways to search for truth: "Everyone who comes to Me, and hears My words, and acts upon them . . . is like a man building a house, who dug deep and laid a foundation upon the rock" (Luke 6:47–48).

Christ says that stability in life is enabled by trust in His Word. But that is not all: We must dig deep in order to lay a foundation upon the rock of God's Word. Many Christians are convinced that God's Word is true theoretically, but they do not put forth the practical effort of digging into God's Word in order to build their lives upon God's bedrock. The benefit of laying our foundation for life upon the Rock is so that "when a flood rose, the torrent burst against that house and could not shake it, because it had been well built" (Luke 6:48b).

The believer who is truly grounded upon God's Word will not be wiped out by the flood of problems that we all face in life. Those who do not have confidence that God's Word is the rock will fail, along with those who have not taken the time or effort to dig down to bedrock. Christ compares "the one who has heard, and has not acted accordingly" to someone who "built a house upon the ground without any foundation; and the torrent burst against it and immediately it collapsed, and the ruin of that house was great" (Luke 6:49).

The authority for the believer is revelation from God—the written Word of God. The God who knows everything tells us some things that we as creatures can know for sure. This provides us with a solid framework for developing a confident perspective for dealing with every area of life, especially those areas on which God has spoken. All truth is based upon God's declaration of reality and His will. Thus, the point of comparative evaluation for the Bible believer is "Thus saith the Lord."

This is why Satan's first challenge against God had to begin with a skeptical challenge of God's Word, "Indeed, has God said," (Gen. 3:1). So we see that we start with either accepting God's Word, which tells us the way things are and should be, or rejecting and questioning God's revelation. People can either work from their own thoughts (rationalism) or with an intuitive feeling (mysticism). For the past two thousand years, the church has cycled between these two erroneous extremes. Robert C. Walton has charted these swings in what he calls "the pendulum effect in church history."[2] Walton labels the two extremes as "emphasis on emotions" (i.e., mysticism) and "emphasis on intellect" (i.e., rationalism), with "biblical Christianity" (i.e., revelation) as the center. Thus, church history has been adrift between the extremes, resulting in reactions from one side and then the other, back and forth from one error to another. There has been little resting in the middle on God's Word.

The two unbiblical approaches of rationalism and mysticism arose early in the history of the church. Marcion (died c. 154) was likely the first rationalist who set reason above revelation. He applied what amounted to a higher critical approach to the New Testament canon and ended up throwing out just about all except the Epistles. Shortly after Marcion came his philosophical opposite, Montanus (c. 170), who developed a mystical form of Christianity that gained wide acceptance within the ranks of the early church. Montanus stressed direct revelation from God, which he added to the New Testament Scripture.

In our own day, the trend, since World War II, has been away from the rationalism of old liberalism that dominated the nineteenth and early twentieth centuries to the mysticism of neo-orthodoxy and the Pentecostal-charismatic movement that continues to grow in influence as we approach a new decade, century, and millennium. The result of this current trend appears to be the death of theology as the primary defining aspect of evangelicalism and fundamentalism. American evangelicalism and fundamentalism were expressions of biblical Christianity that arose to counter liberalism and were primarily built around theology—what one believes. Now *what* one believes is usually relegated to the back seat, and the focus is upon *how* one feels.

David Wells, in *No Place for Truth: Or Whatever Happened to Evangelical Theology?*, has provided the evangelical church with a sober warning about what is now happening Wells observes:

> Without a sharp, cogent, differentiating identity, evangelicals, no less than the Liberals before them, are simply absorbed into the conventions of the modern world in which they live. . . .
>
> [In] this transition from historic Protestantism to modernized evangelicalism, . . . evangelicals who were once cognitive dissidents within the culture are rapidly becoming amicable partners with it. . . . This transition has entailed banishing theology from its place in the center of evangelical life and relegating it to the periphery. Behind this banishment is a greatly diminished sense of truth. Where truth is central in the religious disposition, theology is always close at hand. . . . They are in fact, now beginning to retread the path that the Protestant liberals once trod, and they are doing so, oddly enough, at the very time when many of the descendants of the Liberals have abandoned this path because of its spiritual bankruptcy.[3]

If evangelicals are turning away from theology and God's Word, toward what are they moving? Wells tells us that:

> many of those whose task it is to broker the truth of God to the people of God in the churches have now redefined the pastoral task such that theology has become an embarrassing encumbrance or a matter of which they have little knowledge; and many in the Church have now turned in upon themselves and substituted for the knowledge of God a search for the knowledge of self.[4] . . . In the shift from God to the self as the central focus of faith, in the psychologized preaching that follows this shift, in the erosion of its conviction, in its strident pragmatism, in its inability to think incisively about the culture, in its reveling in the irrational.[5]

Increasingly, in evangelical circles we see this clear trend away from the sufficiency of Scripture to equip believers for the work of the ministry. The pattern is often the same: The Bible does not speak specifically enough in a particular area, so one must develop their views from the secular pool of wisdom. Some examples of areas where we see this trend illustrated are as follows:

- Personal living or sanctification is being replaced by psychology and psychotherapy in an effort to understand the individual rather than God.
- Giving is being replaced by fund-raising programs and marketing.
- Evangelism is being replaced by marketing.
- Christian outreach is being replaced by church growth and sociology in an effort to understand society rather than using God's view of humanity.
- Missions study emphasizes anthropology instead of theology.
- Pastoral theology is being replaced by profession-alism, preoccupation with leadership, and management skills.
- Theological education is being replaced with "how to" training or seminars on all the things we did not learn in seminary.

The leaven of existential idealism and pragmatism is permeating every aspect of the life of the church, often creating a distance between us and sound biblical theology and godly living in much the same way that the rationalism of liberalism challenged our forefathers. During the 1980s and into the 1990s, there appeared to be fewer areas in which evangelicals saw the Bible as speaking authoritatively and sufficiently. This in turn "required" the outside expertise of secular consultants to come to the rescue of the church with "invaluable information," ready to be synthesized into a balanced blend of high-octane "truth." This new evangelical professionalism was often justified by the often-heard slogan that all truth is God's truth, while our leaders seemed to be finding less and less of God's truth in the Bible.

Our evangelical heritage is supposed to be one that follows *sola scriptura* (Scripture alone), as opposed to the authority of the church and the natural theology of Romanism, as well as the authority of human reason and the experience of liberalism. Evangelicals have a place for reason and experience, but it is supposed to be subordinate to Scripture. Paul told the wayward Corinthians that they were to "learn not to exceed what is written" (1 Cor. 4:6). So often evangelicals seem to be caught up in experimentalism, as if God had not given us a clear theological framework from which to interpret every area of life.

In "On Not Whoring after the Spirit of the Age" Thomas C. Oden has noted, "An infatuation with the latest modern ideas has led the church to whore after the spirit of the age and lose its living sense of Christian tradition."[6] Oden sees "four key motifs" at the heart of the problem that is infecting evangelicalism:

1. autonomous individuals
2. narcissistic hedonism
3. reductive naturalism
4. absolute moral relativism[7]

Oden describes the third point as "the view that would reduce all forms of knowing to laboratory experimentation, empirical observation, or quantitative analysis." He notes that reductive naturalism led to the bankruptcy of modern society. Even after such a track record, evangelicals seem to want to bring such things into the church. "It is not time to buy into the ideas of modernity," cries Oden, "for they have been tried and found wanting. Modernity is fully corrupted by its own premises. It is now having to face up to its own interpersonal bankruptcy, social neuroses, and moral vacuity."[8]

## Self-Fulfilling Prophecy
I believe that what Wells has observed within American evangelicalism is an ongoing fulfillment of 2 Timothy 3:1–5:

> But realize this, that in the last days difficult times will come. For men will be lovers of self, lovers of money, boastful, arrogant, revilers, disobedient to parents, ungrateful, unholy, unloving, irreconcilable, malicious gossips, without self-control, brutal, haters of good, treacherous, reckless, conceited, lovers of pleasure rather than lovers of God; holding to a form of godliness, although they have denied its power; and avoid such men as these.

Some structural analysis of this text will help us understand Paul's point. Paul's thesis is that difficult times will be the result of humans loving themselves (v. 2) rather than God (v. 4). The seventeen descriptive words listed in verses 2–4 portray what it means that people have become "lovers of self" instead of being "lovers of God." Paul adds in verse 5 the reason many within the church adopt a narcissistic emphasis of self-love, self-worth, and self-esteem: they hold "to a form of godliness, although they have denied its power." Throughout his writings, Paul relates the power of God to the gospel (cf. 1 Cor. 1–2). This self-virtue will be propagated within the church and will not be based upon the gospel. It will be religious, but it will not be biblical.

A preoccupation with self provides one of the ingredients that support the mystical mind-set. When self is emphasized in such an unbiblical way, then outside influences are often seen to interfere with the pure impressions that spring up from the self. Biblical revelation from outside is often placed below revelation that is produced by the self. Without an external standard such as the Bible provides, one tends to believe that one's own thoughts, feelings, dreams, and impressions are revelation from God. The problem with this kind of religious mysticism is that it adds personal revelations to the Bible, but such revelations are not from God. These personal revelations are "superstitions."

Reconstructionist theologian R. J. Rushdoony has correctly predicted where an emphasis upon self leads:

> Perhaps the clearest area of success in the modern pulpit is in the preaching of psychology. Indeed, it can be said that psychology has in the main replaced theology and the social gospel in most pulpits. Today man is more interested in himself than in God or society.

> Psychology was once a branch of theology, as was anthropology. With the rise of humanism, psychology began to develop new orientations. In the nineteenth century, with Wilhelm Wundt, who was the son of a Lutheran pastor, psychology became the science of experience. Evangelical pietism and scientific experimentalism came together to exalt experience as the new area of reality and truth.

> The exaltation of experience meant that *life* now meant experience; in its truest, fullest sense, the meaning of life was sought in experience, not in God's enscriptured word. Experience became the new means of revelation.

> To cultivate experience means to cultivate also sensitivity to experience.[9]

It is just such a narcissistic selfism that provides the momentum for the modern evangelical church to embrace the mystical approach to Christianity and the Christian life that we see rampant today. At the turn of the twentieth century, the church was battling with rationalism and its implications. Today, as the twentieth century comes to a close, the greater threat is from mysticism. Too many within the church either do not understand its danger, or they do not think that it will negatively impact the life of the church.

In his essay *The Abolition of Man*, C. S. Lewis said that if magic (such as mysticism) and science ever merged, it would produce the greatest deception ever known.[10] He explored this theme in his science fiction novel *That Hideous Strength*. That is what has happened with the recent developments of the New Age movement. And now those influences are all too prominent within the church. In fact, this is what one insightful writer said one hundred years ago when the church was at the height of the rationalist error.

Samuel J. Andrews in his provocative book *Christianity and Anti-Christianity in Their Final Conflict* predicted that the final form of apostasy as the church age came to a close would not be some form of rationalism. Instead, he saw the danger coming from mysticism. In a chapter entitled "The Pantheistic Revolution" Andrews makes the following points in defense of his thesis:

> Yet it may be affirmed in the light both of Scripture prophecy and of the movements and tendencies of the times, that there will be another attempt in Christendom to establish new institutions upon new principles. We may designate it as the Pantheistic revolution, as distinguished from the earlier Atheistic revolution.
>
> In considering this matter, two points present themselves. First, the prevalence of pantheistic principles; secondly, their revolutionary power. . . . We may expect to see Pantheism enlarging its influence in Christendom as Democracy extends. . . . But in Pantheism, the relation of man to God gives a religious tone to all his life, and profoundly affects his relations to others. Because of the common Divinity there is established a more absolute equality between man and man than Democracy can give. . . .

Although based on universalism—the presence of the one Infinite Spirit in all men—it tends to produce an intense individualism or egoism, and a self-exaltation which condemns and resists all legal restraints. Every man, being Divine, is a law to himself. The Divinity in him rules and guides him. He asks nothing from others, he will not be ruled by others, he is sufficient for himself. He owes nothing to the past, no thanks, no reverence.[11]

Andrews provides great insight into the type of mysticism that currently infects the church. Such an emphasis upon self leads to the journey within, that, in a strange way, leads to the *self*-fulfillment of the prophetic overview of the church age.

## Mysticism and Spiritual Warfare

The mentality of metaphysical mysticism has seeped into American evangelicalism, especially into the way that we view Christian life and worship. Metaphysical mysticism affects our ideas about whether God speaks to a believer; spiritual warfare; prophecy, tongues, and healing issues; revivalism; and other matters.

On a trip to California a few years ago, which included a spot on a Christian television program, I was in the studio and watched the taping of a show that featured another guest. The guest was a "Christian psychologist" who was sharing experiences from his practice, which, he said, blends the spiritual with the psychological. He was attempting to bolster his new therapy for treating the "dysfunctional."

The good "doctor" told a story of a Christian woman whom he diagnosed as being demon possessed as a result of something from her past. As he rebuked the evil within her, she was said to have instantly lapsed into a trance during which she went into the birth-labor process. He described the whole delivery performance: the heavy breathing, the cries of pain, and finally the pushing process. The psychologist acted as her coach throughout the whole event, which was being acted out in his counseling office. This episode resulted in five demons, which were said to possess the woman, being exorcised from her through her reliving the act of giving birth.

Stories like this are rapidly becoming commonplace within today's evangelical Christian community. This so-called spiritual warfare involves Christians' casting off the blinders of a Western rational worldview, which for too long has held the church captive, and being awakened to what they consider an enlightened view of the spiritual realm. It seems that almost every aspect of the Christian life is being taught as an aspect of spiritual warfare. I believe that this phenomenon is the result of today's new generation of evangelicals' having adopted a mystical worldview that interprets experiences from a mystical framework instead of from biblical categories.

Arthur L. Johnson in his excellent but neglected book, *Faith Misguided: Exposing the Dangers of Mysticism*, defines and describes mysticism as follows:

> When either the psychological attitude alone, or the more complete philosophical grasp, is translated into theological terms, the resulting view leads the person to equate his inner impressions or subjective states with the voice of God. Such a person, if he is a Christian, tends to believe that the activity of the Holy Spirit within us is expressed primarily through emotional or other noncognitive aspects of our being. Having and "obeying" such experiences is what "being spiritual" is all about.[12]

Johnson's words certainly seem to describe the contemporary bent of evangelical spirituality.

## Mysticism and Spirituality

I believe that there are two basic approaches to spirituality: metaphysical and ethical. Metaphysical spirituality teaches that a believer is directly connected to God and that His Spirit is infused into the believer, much like electricity flows through a motor, energizing to action. It is taught that when a believer sins, the flow stops; when sin is dealt with, the flow resumes. The standard of metaphysical spirituality may or may not involve character development, though it usually focuses on internal experiences and power displays. As this universal mystical view mixed with biblical vocabulary, it developed into an evangelical false teaching.

Ethical spirituality teaches that our relationship with God is mediated indirectly and develops in a way analogous to physical growth. True, Christian growth begins with a direct, metaphysical act of God through the new birth. However, as in physical birth, once conceived and born, the believer is now to use all of the capacity that was imparted at birth to grow through eating (learning the Word) and exercise (obedience), which in turn results in spirituality (i.e., Christlikeness or the fruit of the Spirit). Progress in the spiritual life focuses on ethical progress outside of the believer as he or she measures spirituality in terms of character development.

I believe that every instance of teaching and illustration about spirituality in the New Testament supports the ethical, or growth, approach to sanctification. Yet many evangelicals have taught a blend of both metaphysics and ethics. Perhaps this explains why, in the last few decades, we have seen a steady stream of evangelicals moving toward charismatic spirituality. Ephesians 5:18 is an important passage wherein a metaphysical interpretation has been widely held by evangelicals, but I do not believe that a proper exegesis of the passage will support such an understanding.

What could be called "ethical spirituality" is taught in Ephesians 5:18 and the New Testament epistles. This is evident from an internal investigation of the text. What does the Greek phrase *plērousthe en pneumati,* usually translated "be filled with the Spirit," found in Ephesians 5:18 mean? We must first examine the term *filled (plērēs,* a form of *plēroō).*

*Plērēs* is used six times in the New Testament outside of Ephesians 5:18 in Luke-Acts:

1. Luke 4:1, of Jesus
2. Acts 6:3, of seven men
3. Acts 6:5, of Stephen
4. Acts 7:55, of Stephen
5. Acts 11:24, of Barnabas
6. Acts 13:52, of the disciples (verb form)

These mostly adjectival uses of the word emphasize the *abiding condition* or *state* of fullness that has been achieved. Luke does not present this phrase as a spiritual method or as any kind of special endowment of the Spirit to do a specific task.

The phrase appears to be a way of describing someone who is *already* Spirit-motivated. One does not become "full" in order to achieve a great measure of spiritual motivation, one is spiritually motivated and is *then* described as "full of the Spirit." This is much the same in the case of a man who is exceedingly wise; we describe the greatness of his wisdom by saying "he is full of wisdom." He does not become "full" in order to be wise, but he *is* exceedingly wise and is thus "full."[13]

Notice how Luke's six uses of *filled* clearly stress the abiding result and cannot support the notion of a mystical-infusion kind of filling:

1. Luke 4:1: "Jesus, full of the Holy Spirit, returned from Jordan."
2. Acts 6:3: Seven men "of good reputation, full of the Spirit and of wisdom."

3. Acts 6:5: "Stephen, a man full of faith and of the Holy Spirit."
4. Acts 7:55: Stephen "being full of the Holy Spirit, he gazed intently. . . ."
5. Acts 11:24: Barnabas "a good man, and full of the Holy Spirit and of faith."
6. Acts 13:52: The disciples "were continually filled with joy and with the Holy Spirit."

We see from these uses that a man who is full of the Spirit consistently exhibits a high degree of control by way of the Holy Spirit in his life. This state did not come instantaneously but through a growing process of spiritual maturity. There are no explicit conditions set down in Scripture for this growth. A man full of the Spirit is a spiritually mature man. Therefore, the steps of spiritual maturity would be the means of achieving the end characteristic of fullness. The fullness is not a means for accomplishing an end; it is an end in itself. Timothy Crater says that "one does not become full in order to live the victorious life, but one becomes so submitted to and influenced by the Holy Spirit that the extent of the Spirit's influence over his life may be described by saying 'is full of the Holy Spirit.'"[14] The accomplishment of this state of fullness did not come instantaneously but through a growing process. As long as a person manifests a relatively high degree of the Spirit's control in his or her life, he or she would be characterized by the phrase "full of the Spirit." A young believer or an immature believer may exhibit the Spirit's influence in his or her life but not to a high degree. Spirituality comes through the process of spiritual maturity. The fullness of the Spirit appears to be the normative truth that could be *potentially* true of every follower of Christ.

Luke's use of double objects, such as "full of the Spirit and of wisdom" (Acts 6:3), "full of faith and of the Holy Spirit" (Acts 6:5), "full of the Holy Spirit and of faith" (Acts 11:24), and "filled with joy and with the Holy Spirit" (Acts 13:52) strongly support an ethical or character idea of the filling of the Holy Spirit. Clearly, one does not obtain wisdom, faith, and joy through some form of mystical connection. Thus, since wisdom, faith, and joy are character qualities, that which is linked with them (the Holy Spirit) would also have to be used in the same way.

The only other time the phrase "full of the Spirit" is used in the Greek New Testament is by Paul in Ephesians 5:18. However, the phrase *en pneumati* (by the Spirit) is found also in Ephesians 2:22; 3:5; and 6:18. These all refer to the Holy Spirit as a personal agent, though some hold that the word *spirit* in Ephesians 5:18 refers to the human spirit and not the Holy Spirit. While this is a grammatical possibility, it is not the proper rendering according to the context. The Greek phrase in Ephesians 5:18 does refer to the Holy Spirit because Paul uses this phrase only in reference to the Holy Spirit. The phrase *en eni pneumati* (in one spirit) is found in Ephesians 2:18. But there are no other New Testament references to the filling of the human spirit.

Ephesians 5:18 refers to an ethical filling of the Spirit because the description that follows this command (see 5:19–21) describes the abiding characteristics of a person that are developed over a period of time. These character qualities correspond with Luke's usage in Luke 4:1; Acts 6:3, 5; 7:55; 11:24; and 13:52, as explained above.

In Greek grammar, the nouns have case endings that dictate the way the word is to be used. The *nominative* is the naming case and is the form the subject of a sentence would take. The *genitive* is the case of description and separation. It is usually translated with the prepositions *of* or *from*. Thus, you would have "of the Spirit," denoting the material. The *dative* denotes interest, location, or means; thus, *to*, *in*, and *by*. The *accusative* designates or limits the context to the person or thing being addressed, so it would be the object in the sentence.

It is a rule of grammar that the verb *plēroō* (to fill) takes after it (or governs) more than one case of noun. Each case signifies a distinct translation for the verb. So the *genitive* after *plēroō* refers to the material that fills, the content of the Spirit; the *dative* after *plēroō* refers to the agent or instrument in the filling; the *accusative* after *plēroō* refers to the thing (the human spirit) that is filled. I have come to the conclusion that most English translations incorrectly render the phrase in Ephesians 5:18 as "be filled *with* the Spirit." This would make the English reader think that the genitive case in the Greek is behind this English translation. However, the Greek text uses the dative case. A proper English value for the Greek would be "be filled *by* the Spirit," the dative denoting the agent of the filling, not the content of the filling as the word *with* would lead one to believe. Ephesians 5:18 should be taken in the same way as 2:22: "You are being built together for an habitation of God *by* the Spirit" (author's translation). Thus, it indicates the One who fills, not the content with which one is filled.

What does the filling of the Spirit mean if it does not have a mystical twist, as so many evangelicals advocate? I believe the text teaches the real presence of the Holy Spirit in the believer's life imparted mystically (i.e., directly) at spiritual birth. The force of Paul's exhortation to the Ephesians is that they are to be more and more controlled by the Spirit. That relationship will produce the effects set forth in the Epistle. This does not mean that the Holy Spirit is not involved in the process. He is. However, He is involved in the same way that life animates our physical bodies. So, the fact that we are animated by means of the Holy Spirit, as opposed to the flesh, should produce visible behavior that indicates through the fruit of the Spirit or Christlike character that we are alive spiritually.

The figure of speech that Paul uses here is a *metonymy*, in which the cause is put for the effect, the cause being the Spirit's producing the effects of verses 19–20.[15] The same kind of figure of speech is found in Colossians 3:16, "let the word of Christ richly dwell within you," resulting in the same effects as produced by the Spirit in Ephesians 5:18–20. Here, the agency is the "Word of Christ." In other words, the Spirit enables the believer to produce spiritually mature actions. Just as a person who is alive is enabled by life to act (5:19–21), so the believer who is spiritually alive exhibits the effect. Also, the behavior enabled by the Spirit (i.e., a spiritually alive person) is to be consistent in character with that of God (i.e., the Holy Spirit).

The filling of the Holy Spirit does not mean total control by the Spirit, which would necessitate sinless perfection, since the believer would not be able to resist the sovereign work of God. The filling of the Holy Spirit would not denote "Spirit possession," as some would suggest. If God, the Holy Spirit, completely controlled the person's life, it would be impossible for that person to sin, because God does not sin (James 1:13). Even the decision to thwart the control of the Spirit and fall back under the control of the flesh would be impossible if God were 100 percent in control of the person. Thus, the filling of the Spirit is not total control but rather a progressive and dominant control by the Spirit through one's yielding one's volition to the will of God. When the Spirit controls a person, he or she is described in the New Testament as being full of the Spirit.

Further, the filling of the Holy Spirit emphasizes the effects of the Spirit in one's life (metonymy of cause for effect). Thus, the focus should be on "speaking truth each one with his neighbor" (Eph. 4:25); "being kind to one another, tender hearted, forgiving each other" (Eph. 4:32); "trying to learn what is pleasing to the Lord" (Eph. 5:10); "making the most of your time" (Eph. 5:16); "speaking to one another in psalms and hymns and spiritual songs" (Eph. 5:19–20); and "being subject to one another" (Eph. 5:21).

Paul presents filling as a process that moves toward a goal; thus, it is progressive, not complete or total (cf. Luke 2:40 and John 16:24, which imply progress toward a goal). The goal is the control of the Holy Spirit. This rules out a state of being filled, often coupled with being "in" or "out" of fellowship. An example of this incorrect view is seen in Campus Crusade for Christ's booklet *The Wonderful Discovery of the Spirit-filled Life* (the blue booklet), especially in their concept called "Spiritual Breathing."

The illustration of one's becoming drunk indicates a progressive process. Each drink brings a person closer to drunkenness. When a person is drunk, then we say he or she is full of wine or strong drink. Likewise, when the Spirit gains such control of our lives, others notice that we are full of the Spirit.

The verb *plēroō*, in the form *plērousthe* that is used in Ephesians 5:18, has three implications:

1. *It is plural in number:* "Be all of you filled by the Spirit." This is not a privilege reserved for a few; it is potentially available to all believers.
2. *It is in the present tense:* "All of you be continually filled by the Spirit." The present tense in Greek describes continuing action. Again this fits well with our understanding that this filling is an abiding characteristic of a person's life.
3. *It is a command:* This is not an option. Paul commands us to be spiritually mature, which is the same as saying, "Be filled by the Spirit."[16]

We have seen that the Holy Spirit is the agent of the filling. Further, the Holy Spirit is the One who is working quietly behind the scenes, who has given us the power and ability to live in accordance with Christlike behavior. Christ Jesus is the content, in terms of a *relationship* with Him, that increasingly evidences the fruit of the Spirit. This is seen in the parallel passage to Ephesians 5:18, Colossians 3:15–16. Christ is the content, as spelled out by the Word of Christ (the Bible), so that one can evaluate one's spirituality on the basis of a fixed standard outside of oneself (the Bible) rather than on a subjective and misleading formula. There must be a proper relationship of dependence without legalism and obedience without license to the glory of God. *What does it mean to be filled with the Spirit?* It means to be a mature, Christlike Christian who exhibits the fruit of the Spirit! It means to be occupied with Christ, not with oneself or one's experience with the Spirit as sometimes occurs.

## *End-Time Mysticism*

The New Testament teaches that during the future seven-year tribulation there will come a time of false signs, wonders, and miracles (Matt. 24:4–5, 11; Rev. 13:11–15). At the same time, 2 Thessalonians 2:7 says that "the mystery of lawlessness is already at work" in preparation for the working of the Antichrist, "whose coming is in accord with the activity of Satan, with all power and signs and false wonders" (2 Thess. 2:9). Thus, it is clear that Satan is working in the present age to prepare the world for his program of false mysticism. Such knowledge should lead believers to be on their toes spiritually so that they follow as close as possible the biblical teaching of spirituality. To not do so could mean that even true believers are involved in facilitating the false mysticism of Satan that seems to be spreading like wildfire throughout the church. "Little children, guard yourselves from idols" (1 John 5:21).

# 4

# THE SPIRITUAL WAR FOR THE SOUL OF AMERICA AND THE WEST

## Tim LaHaye

Anyone familiar with Bible prophecy knows that one of the major signs of the "last days" or "the end of the age," as the disciples termed that brief period just prior to the return of Christ (Matt. 24:1–4), is that there will be a time of moral breakdown and degeneracy. The apostle Paul's apt title for that period was "perilous times." He predicated that "in the last days perilous times will come." Then in 2 Timothy 3:1–5 he went on to describe them by listing seventeen tragic characteristics of that period. As you read through them, see how many describe characteristics of our own day:

1. We will be lovers of ourselves.
2. We will be lovers of money.
3. We will be boasters.
4. We will be proud.
5. We will be blasphemers.
6. We will be disobedient to parents.
7. We will be unthankful.
8. We will be unholy.
9. We will be unloving.
10. We will be unforgiving.
11. We will be without self-control.
12. We will be brutal.

13. We will be despisers of good.
14. We will be traitors.
15. We will be headstrong.
16. We will be haughty.
17. We will be lovers of pleasure rather than lovers of God.

Our Lord Himself likened those days just prior to His return as being similar to the days of Noah and the days of Lot (Luke 17:26–30; cf. Gen. 6:1–8; 19:1–17). The days of Noah may have been the most morally degenerate in the history of the world, so the Lord destroyed all but Noah and his family of eight souls. Most Bible scholars feel that the world was so sexually perverted that the world-wide flood became a necessity to preserve the human race. God's destruction of Sodom and Gomorra was for the same reason—to preserve the world from the results of their total sexual perversity. Referring to this period, Jesus said, "Even thus shall it be in the day when the Son of Man is revealed" (Luke 17:30; KJV used throughout this chapter).

Western culture has turned morality on its head and protects by law those who practice the same perverted activities, such as homosexuality, as though these behaviors were normal. Instead, the media and liberal elite, who control the means of communication, castigate those who disapprove of that immoral and often dangerous lifestyle.

The apostle Peter made a similar prediction about "the last days" when he said that people will walk after their own lusts and be scoffers: "Knowing this first, that there shall come in the last days scoffers, walking after their own lusts" (2 Peter 3:3). These people will be blind to the obvious evidence of the creator God and His warnings, but in their rebellion against Him will choose a lifestyle that satisfies their own lusts rather than obey His commands. Who could deny that such is the way of life for most people living in this world? Then, on top of that, we find that the truth as it is in Christ Jesus will be little known in those days. For our Lord said, "I tell you that He will avenge them speedily. Nevertheless, when the Son of Man cometh, shall he find faith on the earth?" (Luke 18:8).

## *Cultural Conditions Will Get Worse*

Cultural conditions will become worse before the Holy Spirit in the church is taken out of this world at the Rapture: "For the mystery of iniquity doth already work: only He who now letteth will let, until he be taken out of the way." (2 Thess. 2:7). Today, the single morally restraining influence in Western civilization is the

Holy Spirit in the church. That is why the world so hates the church—it recalls the days when Western culture at least respected biblical morality; based its laws on it; and presented biblical morality, virtue, and truth as the ideal for social conduct. Today virtue, morality, and truth are trampled in the muck of our lust to do our own thing, and it will probably get worse as we draw closer to the end of this age. Thoughtful people can only imagine what depths of depravity will follow the rapture when the restraining influences in society are removed. Some people believe that the obvious decline of the West is the most important fact of this century. Virtue and integrity are considered unnecessary; perversion is considered honorable; and the family, the universal foundation of all great societies, is in shambles. This tragic decline is not accidental. It is the result of satanic deception.

## *America the Good, a Case Study*

The United States was founded on a uniquely biblical base and, as a result, has enjoyed more freedom for more people for a longer period of time than any other nation in history. Through almost four centuries since the first colonists, the citizens have achieved what no other major nation on earth has for so long. They have elected their own rulers—city, state, and national.

The Protestant Reformation in the early sixteenth century produced a proliferation of Bible translations. The printing press allowed common people to read the Word of God for themselves for the first time in the Christian era. Northern Europe experienced a spiritual revival that invaded their culture and produced the highest standard of civic morality in those countries where the people were most exposed to the Bible.

One thing did not change, however: the people were still subject to the "divine right of kings" or dictators who usurped government control. Government was used (often by ruthless individuals) to dominate their fellow humans while the elite ruling class lived like kings.

In 1620, the first wave of religious volunteers left the tyranny of Europe to come to America to found on this continent "a new nation conceived in liberty." To a previously unknown extent, citizens were enabled to pursue "the right to life, liberty and the pursuit of happiness." These settlers from northern Europe came with the Bible under one arm and a musket cradled in the other, determined to provide a better nation for their children than the ones they had left. The goal was to found society upon human equality and godly moral values.

The unprecedented blessing of God on this new nation was not because of its national resources, its ethnic superiority, or its land surfaces. The country was blessed because its founding fathers, most of whom were from a Calvinist religious tradition, understood human nature and knew it could not be trusted. Consequently, they developed a system of checks and balances for the U.S. Constitution and installed religious freedom in the Bill of Rights. This ensured that no one person could become the king or dictator of our people—every leader was subject to the vote of his constituents or the scrutiny of the constitutionally established body that could depose him if he became too authoritarian or too corrupt.

In addition, America enjoyed the strongest religious roots of any country ever founded, and it is these roots that provided the early laws and policies that have made us a free and morally committed people for the first 250 years of our history. And while we have the greatest Constitution ever written (proven by the fact it has been copied in part or in whole by more countries than any other such document), the Constitution alone did not produce our unprecedented blessings. That honor goes to our religious roots through our churches, our Christian-based schools, and our deeply religious families, many of which had and used Bibles.

What current American historians often forget is that in the century following the founding of Harvard College by John Harvard in 1636, 128 colleges or Bible schools were founded. A religious group, a church, or a body that stood for the propagation of the gospel and the teaching of biblical principles founded each of those schools. Harvard, Princeton, and Yale, all originally religious-based, served as the headwaters of teacher training for the nation's first two centuries. Its graduates were the nation's foremost educators. They imparted the three R's and absolute moral principles of character development arising from a biblical heritage.

George Washington, the president of the Constitutional Convention, knew the importance of the Christian religion to his country. He later observed in his "Farewell Address" that national morality cannot prevail apart from religious principle: "And let us with caution indulge the supposition that morality can be maintained without religion. Whatever may be conceded to the influence of refined education on minds . . . reason and experience forbid us to expect that national morality can prevail in exclusion of religious principle."[1]

John Adams, the second president, said, "We have no government armed with power capable of contending with human passions unbridled by morality and religion. Avarice, ambition, revenge or gallantry would break the strongest cords of our Constitution as a shale goes through a net. Our Constitution was made only for a moral and religious people. It is wholly inadequate to the government of any other."[2]

John Jay, the first chief justice of the U.S. Supreme Court, spoke of the indispensability of the Christian religion and the fact that America was a Christian nation: "Providence has given to our people the choice of their rulers, and it is the duty, as well as the privilege and interest, of a Christian nation to select and prefer Christians for their rulers."[3]

## Religion in America, Fifty Years Later

French scholar and historian Alexis de Tocqueville visited America in 1831. He was so impressed with our culture and constitutional system that he published an exhaustive, two-volume description of our nation that is still popular and available. Some of his observations were:

> On my arrival in the United States the religious aspect of the country was the first thing that struck my attention; and the longer I stayed there, the more I perceived the great political consequences resulting from this new state of religion and the spirit of freedom marching in opposite directions. But in America I found they were intimately united and that they reigned in common over the same country.

> The sects that exist in the United States are innumerable. . . . Moreover, all the sects of the United States are comprised within the great unity of Christianity, and Christian morality is everywhere the same.

> In the United States the sovereign authority is religious, and consequently hypocrisy must be common: but there is no country in the world where the Christian religion retains a greater influence over the souls of men than in America; and there can be no greater proof of its utility and of its conformity to human nature than that its influence is powerfully felt over the most enlightened and free nation of the earth.

> In the United States the influence of religion is not confined to the manners, but it extends to the intelligence

of the people. Among the Anglo-Americans some pro-
fess the doctrines of Christianity from a sincere belief in
them, and others do the same because they fear to be
suspected of unbelief. Christianity, therefore, reigns without obstacle, by universal consent; the consequence is, as
I have before observed that every principle of the moral
world is fixed and determinate, although the political
world is abandoned to the debates and the experiments
of men. Thus the human mind is never left to wander
over a boundless field.[4]

It would be difficult to exaggerate the influence of Bible and
church on the writing of the amazing Constitution of the United
States. An amoral or biblically illiterate people could never have
produced it.

The first three hundred years of United States history was the
religious period of that country. The churches and Christian
thought produced the conscience of the nation. Rights and wrongs
were established by the churches and became the law of the land.
For example, during the first three hundred years of U.S. history,
pornography could be neither bought or sold legally in the U.S.
But in 1972, atheists and secularist judges in the federal court system, up to Supreme Court justices, decided that most antipornog-
raphy statutes violated "freedom of the press." By the end of the
century the nation that once had little pornography had become
the leading porn producer on earth. Not content to contaminate
the minds of North American citizens, the United States contaminated the rest of the world.

### Religious Wars for the Cultural Soul

The unprecedented freedom and prosperity of the U.S. has been
under attack for over two hundred years. I have documented that
attack in *The Battle for the Mind* and *A Nation Without a Conscience*.[5]
As America grew in influence, it was unusually successful in send-
ing its young to the uttermost parts of the earth as missionaries
with the gospel. It is estimated that 85 percent of the evangelistic
work in foreign countries once was done by Christians from the
United States. No wonder Satan declared an unholy war on this
country, its morality, its churches, and its Bible. America was a threat
to his diabolical control of the world—most of which was in the
slavery of government, or in pagan religious practices, which always
have a stifling affect on peace, progress, and freedom.

There is a cultural war between secularism and the church that is rapidly reaching its climax. The war for the soul of our culture is not new. It is the ageless war between God and Satan, between good and evil. All too often, people are the pawns of Satan in this battle. And suffering has been incalculable as a result. Just one of its battlegrounds is armed conflict—international warfare and civil wars. Think how many multiplied millions of people have been killed or maimed in history's fifteen thousand wars.

It is evident that the war for control of world civilization is heating up. Note how many people were killed in the twentieth century, which was supposed at its beginning to be the very climax of civilization. The number of dead in twentieth-century wars totals more than the combined dead of all wars in the history of the world before 1900. Zbignew Brezezinski, former national security adviser to President Jimmy Carter and first executive director of the Trilateral Commission, estimates that perhaps 180 million people were killed by government action in that century—so much for the progress of mankind under the leadership of the secular elite.

What is ironic about all this is that the church of Jesus Christ often acts as if it doesn't even know that there is a war going on. And yet, as we shall see, the Holy Spirit in the church is the first weapon of God in His divine plan of the ages, which includes the present battle for the souls of individuals and the battle for the cultural soul of the world. To any perceptive observer it is obvious, as I shall make clear, that the church is losing the war. God has warned us in prophecy that the church will lose just before He supernaturally intervenes and returns to this earth to forcibly set up His kingdom of righteousness. That kingdom will not only fulfill all the dreams for a cultural utopia but even exceed them. Current world conditions lead both Christians and many secularists to the realization that some kind of supernatural intervention must occur or we will destroy ourselves. But more of that later. For now, to really understand the cultural war we are engaged in, we must go back to its beginning.

## The Tales of Two Cities

Someday I would like to write a book by the title *The Tales of Two Cities,* and show the past, present, and future of the two most influential cities of all time. Jerusalem and Babylon, have served as the working capitols of God and Satan, and the entire world is under the influence of one or the other today.

Jerusalem is the city of God, where He revealed Himself to Abraham, Melchizedek, kings, prophets, and holy men through whom He gave a Holy Book to His followers. This book contained instruction on how they should live their lives, conduct their families, run their country, and enjoy unprecedented freedom and blessing. God's blessing included a morality-based culture. Satan chose Babylon from which to launch his ancient diabolical attack. There he lied to humanity about God, creation, sin, salvation, moral values, culture, and eternity. His primary objective was to get people to worship and serve him. This is why he has introduced idolatrous religions, both polytheistic and naturalistically based on the theory of evolution. It is an attempt to satisfy the God-yearning in the heart of every person. Satan considered that a god who could be seen was more appealing than one who insisted that worshipers never see Him but rather worship Him "in spirit and in truth." Through these religions, he taught that humanity, not God, is "the measure of all things"—the center of his universe. Therefore, anything people want to do is okay. There are no rights and wrongs, nor a hereafter. So eat, drink, and be merry, for tomorrow we die.

Satan's many forms of idolatry, particularly when given supernatural powers by his demons, were so appealing that all but the Christian world has followed them. Thousands of years ago, Nimrod, the founder and originator of this Babylonish religion, was in total rebellion against God. So God confounded the language, causing the people to disburse by language groups all over the world. This is why you can discover some type of Babylonish religion in every religion on earth. In Hindu temples in India and Buddhist temples in China, I have witnessed the modern versions of this Babylonish idolatry that encompasses most of the world.

This original Nimrodism or Babylonish mysticism all happened before God began supernaturally revealing Himself to His creature —man—in and around Jerusalem. In the midst of that idolatry, God raised up Abraham and through him the nation of Israel—the torchbearers of His truth to the world. It was at Jerusalem and through Israel that He revealed His plan to send His only begotten Son into the world to be the divine sacrifice for the human fall and subsequent sin. It was a magnificent plan and was working somewhat, particularly during the kingship of David and his son Solomon. In the latter years of his reign, though, Solomon permitted the nation to worship the idols that his many wives had brought with them. Eventually, the Babylonish worship of the pagan religions supplanted the worship of Jehovah, and Israel adopted the pagan culture and practice instead of following the Lord. It got so bad that God sent judgment on His chosen people by allowing King Nebuchadnezzar to take them captive into Babylon.

## The Return from Babylon

After returning to the land, Israel was so occupied with repairing the damage to their country because of the Babylonian captivity that they did not serve as the torchbearers of Jehovah to the pagan nations of the earth, which was God's original plan for them. While that seventy-year bondage in Babylon did effectively cure Israel of their penchant for idolatry, it did not cure them of their rebellion and self-will. During that period, named by Bible scholars the silent years between the testaments when they had no writing prophets and few spiritual leaders, Satan and his demons filled that vacuum with polytheistic religions in Eastern culture and the spread of the Hellenistic philosophy of humanism in Western culture.

## The Period of Jesus

When Jesus Christ came into this world, it was filled with either heathen paganism based on idolatry from Babylon or godless Greek humanism, which masqueraded as philosophy. Greek humanism was then, and is today in its secular religious form, humanity's best attempt to solve its problems independent of God. Wherever humanism and idolatry prevail, personal freedom is lost, family values and morality are despised, womanhood degenerates, and the worship of the true God is forbidden or ridiculed.

Into such a pagan world, Jesus Christ, God's own Son, came to die for sin. His sinless, miraculous, and sacrificial life was climaxed by the miracle of His bodily resurrection, earning Him a unique position in history. It is fitting that time has been separated into two eras—"before Christ," B.C. and "in the year of our Lord," A.D. Jesus Christ is the one person who stands head and shoulders above each of the other 12 billion people who has ever lived. No one else comes close. No one else has so influenced education, religion, music, art, culture, the status of women, and personal freedom. Where Jesus Christ and His teachings have been allowed, culture has been elevated morally. Jesus made this level of impact on the world in only three years. Obviously, He could not have been just a man. He was literally what He said and what the prophets and apostles said He was—the Son of God.[6]

The most significant thing Jesus did after His resurrection was to establish the church. This altered the course of the world more than any other event in history. He predicted that the gates of hell could not stand against his people (Matt. 16:18). In three hundred years, that initial body of believers spread all over the world. By A.D. 325, it was the recognized church of the Roman Empire.

Those Christians of the first three centuries were driven by the conviction that their Lord could return at any time. That challenge permeates the New Testament and continues to drive the true church that takes the Scriptures literally and believes that Christ could come in its lifetime. In the case of the early church, they were so filled with the expectation of the at-any-moment return of their Savior that they filled the whole world with their message while leading millions to faith in Christ. In spite of unprecedented persecution, by A.D. 312, millions had converted to Christianity.

## Conversion of Constantine

Even Constantine, the Roman emperor, professed faith in Christ and adopted Christianity as the state religion of Rome. While historians involve themselves with whether Constantine accepted Christ for political reasons, they often lose sight of the incredible achievement of those first three hundred years. Jesus made the churches, according to Revelation 1–3, the lampstands of the world, and He is seen walking, through His spirit, among the lampstands. He commanded them, and us, to be the light of the world. During the initial three hundred years, Satan was busy moving his headquarters. After the fall of the Babylonian Empire, he had moved his headquarters first to the city of Pergamum, where Revelation 2:13 tells us Satan was seated, and then to idolatrous Rome, the governmental capital of the world for five hundred years.

The most significant thing about the date 312 is that in the tale of two influential cities in the great war between God and Satan for the soul, it had taken just three hundred years for early Christianity to conquer the spiritual city of Babylon. That means that just over eight hundred years after Satan's pagan city of Babylon had conquered God's city of Jerusalem and had taken its leaders captive, the early church of Jesus Christ had spiritually conquered Rome. That doesn't mean that every citizen of Rome was a Christian, but for a brief time the majority of the population was Christian. Little did the fourth-century Christian leaders who moved the headquarters of the church to Rome realize that they were moving right into the very headquarters of spiritual Babylon. Eventually that proved to be the undoing of the church.

## Allegorizing the Bible

Augustine is also responsible, due to his allegorizing of Scripture, for opening the door of the church to pagan idolatrous practices that eventually changed the Church of Rome, which today is more Babylonish than it is Christian. In addition, he brought enough of his residual Greek philosophy into the church that it ultimately made the church (through its colleges and universities) the teachers of Greek humanism. Eventually, this helped to produce secular humanism, which is the official religious philosophy of secular America today (as well as almost every other Western culture). Thomas Aquinas (1225–1274), a theologian and Greek scholar who was canonized by the Church of Rome, followed a long line of advocates of Augustine's teaching. Aquinas did more to revive interest in the writings and thought of Aristotle than he did to promote the teaching of Scripture. While he personally held that the Scriptures were inspired and held them in high esteem, he also elevated the philosophy and writings of Aristotle, because he considered true learning to be a balance of both wisdom and Scripture. Only a short time after Aquinas's death, Rome's theologians elevated Aristotle and Greek philosophy above Scripture for Scholastic Europe. The resulting tradition was part Greek philosophy, part Babylonish paganism, and some Scripture. Today, knowledgeable theologians will admit that the official teaching of the Church of Rome is based on fifteen hundred years of tradition and Scripture —and, I might add, the infallibility of the popes. Much of the Church's teaching was totally unscriptural. By not accepting the early church's doctrine of *sola scriptura*, Catholic and then other universities and colleges opened the door to skepticism and secularism.

## The Dark Ages

The medieval world, from around 400 to 1500, were spiritual dark ages, and the people lived in unending ignorance and poverty because the Bible was kept from them. The official policy of the Roman Church was to claim that Bibles should be only in monasteries, studied by priests and scholars who could interpret it properly. Schools were nonexistent, and during much of that time only one person out of twenty thousand could read. Even if they had known how to read, however, the Bible was available only in Greek and Latin—two languages little known by most Europeans. The Bible had little influence on Western culture during much of that eleven hundred years.

## The Bible and Reformation

At the same time, however, valiant saints both inside and outside the Roman Church fought bravely to release the Word of God from its ecclesiastical prison. Men such as John Wycliffe (1330–1384), "the morning star of the Reformation," lived and wrote in great uncertainty about their safety. Jan Hus (1373–1415) was one of thousands burned alive; William Tyndale (c. 1494–1536) was strangled; others were beheaded. These martyrs died for translating and preaching from translated versions of the Bible—Bibles available to common people in their own language. In so doing, they changed the face of Europe, then America, then many countries through cross-cultural evangelization. The effect that the Bible has had on people of all walks of life has truly been miraculous. Even in "the post-Christian era," no other book comes close to influencing people as has this international best-seller. The only time the Bible does not influence people or culture is when it is kept closed or under glass in museums, so that it cannot be read and studied by the common people to whom God addressed His words.

Martin Luther, who touched off the Europe-wide Reformation, is best known for the Ninety-five Theses he nailed on the Wittenberg church's door and by the church denomination that bears his name. He should also be recognized for pioneering the training of the young. He realized that to influence the next generation there must be a literate people, and he did his best to educate the children of Germany, the lowlands, and Scandinavia and to provide them with a Bible-based philosophy of life. The influence of his schools on the future generations of Germany was incredible. John Calvin, another leader of the Protestant reformation copied the church-related schools' technique for teaching the Bible and Christian doctrine to the next generation, thus preparing a literate clergy for the new Protestant churches that were springing up.

One of the inventions at that time that changed the world, beginning with Christians, was the printing press. The first book printed with movable type was the Bible. Then Christian literature, Bible translations, tracts, and religious books began to appear, leaving a powerful impact on Europe, where culture and civilization took many leaps forward.

But Satan was not asleep during this period. He had René Descarte (1596–1650) and other skeptical philosophers, many of them turned off by the decadent conditions in the church of "Babylon," which had a stranglehold on much of the politics in Europe. Actually, since the days before Aquinas, Satan had been sowing skepticism and humanistic philosophy in the new universities of Europe. French skepticism and even German rationalism was an outgrowth of this training of skeptics in religious educational institutions. François-Marie Voltaire (1694–1778), Jean-Jacques Rousseau (1712–1778), G. W. F. Hegel (1770–1831), and many others who had such an influence on shaping the Enlightenment, an antibiblical philosophy, prepared the way for the French

Revolution and the socialistic philosophy that swept like wildfire through the academic institutions, the arts, governments, and journalism.

## Fifty-Year Cultural Decline

Many times during the period of human history, Satan has been poised to launch his final strike against humankind. But there is an obvious power greater than Satan that seems to wait until the last moment, and then he strikes. Whether it is through Noah and his ark, the judges of Israel, or the return of the children of Israel to their homeland (not once but twice), God is still in control when things seem to be out of control. We could be on the verge of another divine intervention today—possibly the Rapture of the church followed by the seven-year tribulation that culminates with the final victory of Christ over Satan. This series of events will precede the thousand years of peace that both the prophets and the apostles predicted. If so, it had better happen soon, or Satan will take over this world.

Of one thing I am certain: Western culture, including North America and Europe, cannot sustain fifty years of decline as precipitous as the fifty we have just ended. I have been in the ministry now for fifty years. During that time, I have seen moral decay to a state that would have been unimaginable fifty years ago. Today, 250,000 guns are taken to schools each year. Rape, murder, and other forms of violence have invaded the once-quiet halls of learning. Our streets used to be safe for women after dark. How can they get much more dangerous than they are today? Radio programs and movies could not even use the word *damn* without causing community outrage; today unprintable four-letter words are common fare. Every person who watches the evening news or a prime-time television program can easily add to the list. These changes are appearing in the media not only in the West but also in all developing nations of the world.

Someone has said in half-jest that medieval people were so inhumane as to put mentally challenged people on stage for sport, while twentieth-century society put them on television and in the highest positions of government, media, and education. We may laugh at their amoral and immoral antics, but they are destroying our culture. The true church of Jesus Christ is still saltlike enough to be a restraining, preserving influence. The media has no conscience and is all but totally in the control of Satan and his willing followers. Unfortunately, the media has more influence on our culture than does the church. Ted Turner, one of the most influential media moguls of our day told me personally fifteen years ago, "Television is more powerful than the government—it elects the government!"

## *Is There Hope for the U.S.?*

Deadness easily describes the spiritual climate of Europe; I still believe that, if the Lord waits to return, He yet has a plan to use the United States to win many to Christ. Let me share four reasons for such hope.

First, our God is merciful. Even the rebellious prophet Jonah knew God was merciful, for he said, "I knew that thou art a gracious and compassionate God, slow to anger and abundant in lovingkindness, and one who relents concerning calamity" (Jonah 4:2). If God had dealt with this country on the basis of what we deserve, we would have ceased to be a nation long ago.

Even as morally dark as America is today, we could yet experience a moral and spiritual revival—not because we deserve it, but because God is a merciful God and abundant in lovingkindness. Just as He spared wicked Nineveh in the days of the prophet Jonah, so He may yet spare America. As God Himself said, "And should I not have compassion on Nineveh, the great city in which there are more than 120,000 persons who do not know the difference between their right and left hand, as well as many animals?" (Jonah 4:11).

If God would save Nineveh because of 120,000 innocent boys and girls, who didn't know their left hand from their right, why would He not also save America? We have 47 million children, many of whom "don't know their right hand from their left" or don't know right from wrong. They have been brainwashed by secularists who teach them that there are no moral absolutes.

I believe that our merciful God will yet spare America because of who and what He is. But there is another reason for which He will yet spare us—a principle of His Word that He has honored for over three thousand years: the Abrahamic covenant.

Second is the Abrahamic covenant. Many people believe that God will save America because of the promise that God made to Abraham. God performed a biological miracle on the bodies of Abraham and Sarah and created a new nation of people that eventually came to be called the Hebrews, and then the Jews. A part of God's promise was, "And I will make you a great nation, and I will bless you, and make your name great; and so you shall be a blessing; and I will bless those who bless you, and the one who curses you I will curse. And in you all the families of the earth shall be blessed" (Gen. 12:2–3; cf. 27:29; Num. 24:9).

One of our nation's worthwhile accomplishments has been its consistent regard for the plight of the Jewish nation. No nation in the history of the world has a better record of treating individual Jews with respect than does America. The same can be said for our befriending Israel as a nation. America has committed many sins, for which we may well deserve judgment, but as a nation, we have been a consistent friend of the Jews and the nation of Israel.

Many nations have been evil to the Jews and have suffered as a result. Some may claim that this is a coincidence; others see a clear purpose of God in it. England declined as a world power over the very period in which they did not honor the Balfour Declaration and conspired with the Arab nations against the infant nation. Before them were France, Spain, and Italy. Czarist Russia fell after hideous pogroms. The Soviet Union likewise collapsed under its own weight after many years of mistreating the Jews.

America, by contrast, has been a benefactor for the Jewish state. In 1948, President Harry Truman helped persuade the United Nations to recognize Israel as a nation. Since then, the United States has contributed more than $50 billion of foreign aid to that state. Without U.S. protection, the nation of Israel probably would not exist. If we have any basis for expecting God to bring a revival to America, it is because we have consistently been good to Israel.

Third, the hand of providence is strong in the United States. God has spared the nation because, as the framers of the Constitution believed in 1789, His hand was on the founding of the nation. Anyone familiar with the history of this country knows that it is a miracle nation. Without "the strong hand of Providence," as George Washington called it, we would never have survived in the first place. Among the first settlers were Puritan Pilgrims who would never have survived that first long, cold winter without divine intervention.

Recently, we took our granddaughter to the site on the Delaware River where God supernaturally arranged a fog through which General Washington led seven thousand troops and eighteen hundred wounded soldiers to safety during a British siege that would have effectively destroyed any chance of winning the Revolution against Britain. The fledgling country's victory was a miracle, as have been so many other war victories. God had a plan for the nation, and a great part of His plan, no doubt, involved using the United States as a beacon and bearer of the gospel. No other country has so cooperated with God's worldwide plan to spread the gospel to "the remotest part of the earth" (Acts 1:8).

Politically, the U.S. has inspired freedom-loving people throughout the earth. I believe that the country has yet to fulfill her destiny. To do so, however, the U.S. must reverse its moral decline.
Otherwise, it will plunge deeper into the Sodom and Gomorra
designed by secular humanistic, liberal socialists. As North Americans
in the United States and Canada have ignored God and expelled
Him from public schools, the nations have declined spiritually and
morally. I pray God will send one more great revival as He has
done before.

For a revival to have any lasting effects, U.S. citizens will have
to promote legislative reform to undo the harm the secularists have
done to their nation. Otherwise, a revival will be short-lived. Liberal secularists have legislated immorality into the culture for fifty
years; it must be overturned by new legislation that restores traditional moral values in the public square. That will require about 30
percent more elected officials committed to such values during the
next thirty to fifty years. The nation needs a Supreme Court led by
men and women who enforce the Constitution as the Christian
forefathers wrote it, not as liberal atheists wish it to be. Changing
the makeup of the Supreme Court will take at least twenty years.

Fourth, though other nations have more evangelical Christians
*per capita,* there still are more Christians in actual numbers in the
United States than in any other country on earth. During God's
conversation with Abraham, found in Genesis 18, God agreed to
spare Sodom and Gomorra if He could find within it ten righteous
souls. Ten could not be found. And despite the glaring evils of the
nation, no other major country has so many Spirit-filled, Bible-
believing Christians. However people today define the term, the
George Gallup organization tells us that 60 million or 70 million
U.S. people still claim to have been "born again." Could those
among this number who actually are born again be preserving
America from God's destruction? The judging hand of God has
never fallen on any nation that had so great a presence of Christians. Consequently, we do not think God will destroy the U.S.,
though we certainly can expect heavy discipline. Nations, as individuals, can rarely be trusted with great blessing. The "good life"
in America is not conducive to faith in God. In the Old Testament,
Israel had that problem. That is why they went through the cycles
of spirituality described in the book of Judges. They strayed from
God's moral values. God sent a nation to humble them. God heard
their cry and sent a deliverer.

The future of North America—and subsequently the rest of the world—will likely be decided in the coming decades of the twenty-first century. It is a time for great prayer dependence and energetic work. We also need to urge Bible-believing pastors in every free nation to teach citizenship responsibilities. Christians should vote for the most morally committed candidates. In U.S. elections, for example, only 30 to 48 percent of Christians vote—depending on the election. When they do, about 80 percent or more vote for the more morally committed candidate—regardless of party affiliation. Because Christians are the largest minority in the nation (61 million who identify themselves as "born-again"), only another 20 percent need to go to the polls to elect enough new leaders who share Christian values and will work to reverse the moral decline.

Personally, I believe that the future of the United States is in the hands of the pastors. If enough of them take seriously their Christian citizenship responsibilities as they do their evangelistic responsibilities, we could turn this country back to a better moral foundation within two decades. The church needs to evangelize, pray, and vote to reverse Satan's fifty-year destruction of our culture. Only the church, with God's help, can save America. It is up to our nation's pastors to lead their congregations to pray, evangelize, and vote—as if the future of America is in our hands, for it is!

The twenty-first century could see a return to moral sanity in our country if our pastors would use the evangelistic alter, the prayer meeting, and the ballot box as tools for much-needed reform.

We owe our God and our children no less!

# 5

# THE SHIFTING RELATIONSHIP BETWEEN CHURCH AND STATE

## Paul R. Fink

In the new millennium, how does government relate to religious and church autonomy? Will evangelicals have to go underground in order to worship God as they please? What can we expect from both democratic and despotic nations around the world?

The last decade of the twentieth century saw some of the most blatant persecution against believers since the Reformation. Thousands of Christians died for their faith. China continued to persecute Christians, with many confined to prison for their public proclamation of the gospel. And though the communist empire collapsed, state Orthodox churches in Russia and other small independent countries manipulated the government to place almost unbearable restrictions on evangelical assemblies.

Christianity in the United States was not exempt from assault by anti-Christian groups—especially those advancing the homosexual lifestyle. Thus, there was both good news and bad news. The good news was that the California Supreme Court refused to hear an appeal by a homosexual who was forced out as a leader of the Boy Scouts of America. The bad news was that gay rights groups in other states sued the Scouts for discrimination against homosexuals. Will the government cave in to the liberal bullies?

Though small victories have been won, the assault continues against Christians and biblical morality. In Waco, Texas, a sexual-abstinence program was rejected by the local school board because it teaches morality. Those who objected to the program claimed that the issue was about separation of church and state since the program utilizes biblical standards of ethics.

In A.D. 2000 and beyond, how will state educational commissions treat those who home school as well as Christian private schools? States are becoming more adversarial toward Christian education. States are arguing before federal courts that any decision made by a Christian parent that runs contrary to what the state deems best places the child in a disadvantaged environment. Soon, in some states, credits earned by those who have been home schooled will not be accepted in colleges and universities.

Church tax-exempt status has not escaped scrutiny either. In America, we teeter on the brink concerning this issue. As of this writing, churches are still given the blessing of tax exemption, but what will happen in future decades as our government becomes more secular and Christian institutions appear to be more expendable?

## *Questions to Consider*

In discussing the relationship of church to state in this chapter, the concept of the church will be broadened to include the individual believer. The topic, then, might be redefined as the relationship or the responsibility of believer to state. We will ask three questions that, when answered, set forth the relationship or responsibility of the believer to the state:

1. What is the Old Testament teaching concerning the state's authority?
2. What is the New Testament teaching concerning the state's authority?
3. In what realms is the believer responsible?

It is to the first of these questions that attention is now directed.

### Old Testament Teaching and State Authority

The seed of human government begins wherever authority is vested. This vesting of authority is first seen in the Old Testament in the Noahic covenants. But there also are other views of authority observed in God's instructions in Eden and in His directives following the Fall.

*The Instructions in Eden: Genesis 1:28–2:17.*

Before the Fall, Adam is ordered to (1) populate the earth (1:28), (2) subdue the earth (1:28), (3) exercise dominion over the animal creation (1:28), (4) care for the Garden of Eden and enjoy its fruit (1:29; 2:15), and (5) refrain from eating the fruit of the tree of the knowledge of good and evil under penalty of death (2:16–17). While the focus of this period is not human government, the following relevant factors can be observed.

Adam and Eve, obviously, were the first human beings to inhabit the earth. They arrived on the scene by direct divine creation. However, God charged them with the responsibility to be fruitful, and multiply, and fill the earth (Gen. 1:28a). Implicit within this command is Adam's responsibility for the society that would develop from his obedience. He would hold this position by virtue of his obedience to God's command. It is an interesting aside to observe that this is the *only* command that God gave man that man has *willingly* tried to obey!

The Edenic period lays out the scope of human government. Adam is ordered to subdue the earth and "have dominion over the fish of the sea, and over the fowl of the air, and over every living thing that moveth upon the earth" (Gen. 1:28b). Had the Fall never taken place, Adam would still have had a responsibility to discharge. As the head of God's creation, he was to cultivate the earth and maintain his dominion over God's creatures—fish, fowl, and every living thing upon the earth. Had the Fall not taken place, Adam could have maintained this role forever. However, with the entrance of sin and death, Adam's headship and dominion was necessarily carried on by his successors and ultimately formalized in the institution of human government that would be responsible for its care of God's earth and his creatures.

This pre-Fall period laid out the initial responsibility of humans to government. Genesis 2:15–17 states:

> Then the LORD God took the man and put him into the garden of Eden to cultivate it and to keep it. And the LORD God commanded the man, saying, "From any tree of the garden you may eat freely; but from the tree of the knowledge of good and evil you shalt not eat, for in the day that you eat from it you shall surely die.

God puts definite restrictions upon the man to whom He has given responsibility over His creation. Humankind was given responsibility to dress and keep the garden and was given restrictions as to what they could and could not eat. Had sin not entered the world, these responsibilities and restrictions would have continued forever. With the entry of sin and death, God terminated these responsibilities, because humankind was banished from the garden. The responsibility to care for creation and creatures ultimately was given to the institution of human government.

*Following the Fall: Genesis 3:14–21.*

The concept of responsibility to God for the care of His creation and creatures did not cease with the time in the garden. Indeed, it is continued in the early directives made to Adam (Gen. 3:14–21) in which God sets forth the conditions that will prevail from the time of the Fall until Christ comes to set up His kingdom upon this earth. There are ten provisions that follow the Fall:

1. The serpent is cursed; it must crawl on its belly (3:14).
2. Satan is judged; he will enjoy limited success (3:15).
3. The first prophecy of the coming of Messiah is given (3:15).
4. There will be multiplication of conception; necessitated by the introduction of death into the human race (3:16).
5. There will be pain in childbirth (3:16).
6. There will be an increase in woman's sexual desire; necessitated by natural hesitancy due to the pain incurred in childbirth (3:16).
7. The woman is made subject to her husband (3:16b).
8. The ground is cursed and will bring forth weeds among the food that humans must eat for their existence (3:17–18).
9. Humans will perspire; an anatomical change will take place (3:19).
10. Humans died spiritually and die physically; flesh returns to dust, from which it was originally taken (3:19).

Humans continue to be responsible to God and exercise dominion over God's creation and creatures by virtue of God's command. This headship and dominion will be passed on to Adam's successors and will ultimately be formalized in the institution of human government.

## The Noahic Covenant: Genesis 9:1–17

The Noahic covenant includes God's blessing upon Noah and his family (9:1a), God's general revelation of His covenant to Noah and his family (9:1b–7), and God's specific revelation of His covenant with Noah (9:8–17). While the Noahic covenant is concerned with much more than the origin of human government and its authority, many insights can be gained from a consideration of applicable parts of that covenant.

The Noahic covenant spells out governmental authority. God's general revelation of His covenant to Noah and his family concerns (1) his progeny (9:1b), (2) dominion over creation (9:2), (3) food (9:3–4), (4) capital punishment for beast and humans (9:5–6), and (5) an additional word concerning his progeny (9:7). It is the revelation concerning capital punishment that provides the clue to the origin of human government and its responsibility. In that revelation God states, "And surely I will require your lifeblood; from every beast I will require it. And from every man, from every man's brother I will require the life of man. "Whoever sheds man's blood, by man his blood shall be shed, for in the image of God He made man" (Gen. 9:5–6).

Three times in this text God says, "I will require it" (lit. "require or demand an accounting"). Thus, it is God who demands an accounting of human government for its protection of life.

The Noahic covenant specifies the recipients of governmental authority. The text indicates that every human being or animal who sheds a person's blood will be held accountable. There are to be no more Cains (cf. Gen. 4:8–15), but the shedding of an animal's blood (9:4) should not cause us to be indifferent to bloodshed. Whenever a person's blood is shed, whether by another person or by a beast, God demands an accounting of it. The agency held accountable is human government.

Governmental authority is assigned by the Noahic covenant. Genesis 9:6 explains 9:5 and shows how God demands that the accounting for human blood be done. He lets humankind be the avenger through the institution of human government—the basic institution for the welfare of humans. Since humankind is given the power over the highest good that it possesses (i.e., life), humans also have power over the lesser things (i.e., property for taxes and his or her person for service).

The covenant asserts that government authority is just. The expression "his blood shall be" is not a simple future tense. It is a *niphal* imperfect that is best understood to have the sense of an imperative, i.e., "by man his blood *must* be shed." Capital punishment on the part of human government is not a matter of choice or preference—it is a divinely ordained command. To fail to exercise it (whether on an individual or a national scale) flaunts God's command. Those who would tamper with this law are trying to be wiser than the Lawgiver and to overthrow the pillar of safety that He has provided for the welfare of humankind. While it is possible to understand this responsibility to be individual because when the command was given only Noah and his family were alive on the earth's surface, it is important to realize that it was God's intention for this responsibility to be continued in perpetuity. Human government is the only institution capable of discharging this responsibility.

Therefore, the Noahic covenant vindicates governmental authority. The reason authority is an absolute necessity is because "in the image of God made he man." This shows the value of humans in God's sight. God does not require an accounting of humankind for the shedding of an animal's blood, but he does require an accounting when humankind's blood is shed whether by person or animal.

## Questions Concerning Governmental Authority

From the exegetical considerations of this passage, at least four logical and commonly asked questions arise:

*First, doesn't this command conflict with "Thou shalt not kill" (lit. murder) of the Mosaic Law?*

No. Humans are here given (governing) power over human life. The Ten Commandments deal with personal morality. With Noah, official conduct is in view. A person has the right to take another person's life in the capacity of human government.

*Second, isn't capital punishment cruel and inhumane punishment?*

No. The concept can best be explained by an illustration. If a physician's patient has cancer, the physician dons his surgical garments, takes surgical instruments in hand, and cuts into the patient's body. His cutting actually injures the patient and makes him very ill. Is the physician cruel? No! He is actually praised for injuring his patient's body because in so doing he has cut out the cancerous growth that would otherwise destroy the rest of the body. So it is with capital punishment. If the "cancer" is not destroyed and cut out, it will destroy the rest of the body.

*Third, what about corruption in human government?*

God does not hold the individual responsible as an individual for the corruption of human government. He does hold the individual responsible for obeying Him, however.

For example, if one is called to serve on a jury, the believer has the Holy Spirit within to guide him or her in coming to a verdict. If, under the control of the Holy Spirit, the believer believes the defendant to be guilty of murder, then he or she must vote for capital punishment. If under the control of the Holy Spirit the believer believes the defendant to be innocent, he or she must stand for what he or she believes to be the truth, even if this "hangs the jury."

*Fourth, what about wars?*

Wars are an extension of the command to have capital punishment.

In war, one human government executes capital punishment upon another nation that has offended. A soldier who kills in the line of duty is acting as God's agent. He is not guilty of murder. He is acting in an official capacity.

## Summary

From Genesis 9:1–17, it can be seen that human government originated with God's command to Noah following the universal flood. At that time, God specifically gave to humans, in the corporate form of human government, the responsibility for the avenging of human blood when it is shed by either another human or an animal. This represents the epitome of the authority of human government and also constitutes the authority for human government's power in all the lesser realms of society, as is plain in later New Testament revelation.

### Governmental Authority in the New Testament

At least three outstanding New Testament people recognized governmental authority—Jesus, Paul, and Peter.

#### Jesus: Matthew 22:21

If anyone could have claimed immunity from the authority of human government, it would have been Jesus. In His conflict with the Herodians and in response to their question as to whether it was lawful to give tribute to Caesar, Jesus replied, "Render to Caesar the things that are Caesar's; and to God the things that are God's" (Matt. 22:21b). Jesus clearly delineates between two realms of obligation for each human being—government and religion. There is a difference between the Herodians' question and Jesus' answer. They asked whether it was lawful to *give* (as a gift) tribute to Caesar. Jesus' response is that one should render (by obligation to give) to Caesar. Giving to Caesar is not in the realm of a voluntary gift. The eternal obligation to God does not discharge one from the temporal obligation to support the government financially. Paul amplifies this concept in Romans 13.

#### Paul: Romans 13:1–7.

Paul writes the definitive word regarding the believer's relationship to government in Romans 13:1–7:

> Let every person be in subjection to the governing authorities. For there is no authority except from God, and those which exist are established by God. Therefore

he who resists authority has opposed the ordinance of God; and they who have opposed will receive condemnation upon themselves. For rulers are not a cause of fear for good behavior, but for evil. Do you want to have no fear of authority? Do what is good, and you will have praise from the same; for it is a minister of God to you for good. But if you do what is evil, be afraid; for it does not bear the sword for nothing; for it is a minister of God, an avenger who brings wrath upon the one who practices evil. Wherefore it is necessary to be in subjection, not only because of wrath, but also for conscience' sake.

From this passage six facts are evident:

*First, there is the overall principle of subjection.* Subjection to the government—whether local, county, state, or federal—is not optional. It is an absolute necessity for Christian and non-Christian alike. Christians should be the best citizens that the government has. It is important to realize that when he wrote these words, Paul was under Emperor Nero's rule and that Nero was noted for his persecution and murder of Christians.

*Second, the origin of governmental authority is God.* The authorities that exist have been established by God (lit. have been, are, and will be put into place by God). There is not a ruler, whether elected or usurped, who came into power by his own means or initiative. No politician is smart enough and no dictator is strong enough to put himself in power. God always has been, always is, and always will be the one who puts individuals into the leadership in keeping with His plan. Therefore, whenever a person resists government or governmental leaders, he or she is in opposition to what God has instituted. Such rebellion will not prevail. When it comes to "Christian civil disobedience," some cite the apostles (cf. Acts 5:18–29, "We ought to obey God rather than men"). The religious leaders who had forbidden the apostles to preach in the name of Jesus, however, imprisoned them. Rome just provided the jail facility. The apostles were not flaunting civil authority. Rather, they refused to obey a false religious authority that had no authority over them. Those who disobey human government will bring judgment on themselves.

*Third, the purpose of governmental authority is to preserve moral order.* The state is to be the judge of right and wrong as it determines what right and wrong is. It is to judge the wrong and approve the right. If the state fails to do this, *it* is disobedient to God. Right and wrong are determined by the state, and ideally the state should get its values from God. Often it does not. This is why it is important for Christians to be involved in governmental processes. A governmental leader is actually God's servant (*diakonos*, lit., deacon, servant, minister of God), if only they realized that fact! Three principles emerge from Romans 13:3–4: (1) Christians should respect government; (2) Christians should obey the government; and (3) Christians should expect punishment for disobeying the government. The sword is a symbol that represents the authority given to government to protect itself by punishing those who do what it has determined is wrong. God has not only given government the responsibility to uphold the right and avenge the wrong but also the authority to do it.

*Fourth, Christians should obey government.* The Christian's subjection to government is necessary, not optional. This subjection is to be motivated not only because of possible punishment—though such fear is a legitimate reason for obedience—but also because of conscience (i.e., a consistent Christian testimony).

*Fifth, Christians should support the government financially.* Taxes (*phorous*) are paid to support the governmental authorities because they are God's servants (*leitourgoi*, lit., "liturgist," a religious priestly term) and give their full time to governing. That is how they serve God!

*Sixth, Christians should support governmental officials appropriately.* Taxes (*phorous*) are paid to support the government official's salary. Revenue (*telos*) are tolls paid for use of government facilities such as roads, bridges, and utilities. Respect (*phobon*, "fear") is reverential awe for the one who has power entrusted to him or her. Honor (*timēn*, "honor") is the reverence and respect due to one who holds office.

*Peter: 1 Peter 2:13–17.*

Peter's teaching concerning the Christian's responsibility to the state in 1 Peter 2:13–17 supplements Paul's:

> Submit yourselves for the Lord's sake to every human institution, whether to a king as the one in authority, or to governors as sent by him for the punishment of evildoers and the praise of those who do right. For such is the will of God that by doing right you may silence the ignorance of foolish men. Act as free men, and do not use your freedom as a covering for evil, but use it as bondslaves of God. Honor all men; love the brotherhood, fear God, honor the king.

Peter makes two assertions concerning the Christian's responsibility to the state:

*First, God commands our subjection to the state.* In principle, this applies "to every human or social institution" *(pasē anthrōpinē ktisei)*. Such institutions include the state, the household, or the family. This is to be done for the Lord's sake ("because of the Lord's example or because of the Lord's cause," the Christian cause).

Jesus' life was one of obedience. He showed respect to Pilate and commanded His people to obey those in authority over them. He placed Himself in complete subjection to Caiaphas and Herod. Pacifists in our century have damaged the Lord's cause by failing to recognize the difference between religion (spiritual) and state (governmental). As long as the state is legislating within its God-ordained realm, the believer is to be in subjection to it and to obey its laws. However, if the state tries to legislate in the realm of the spiritual, the believer is to obey God rather than the state (cf. Acts 5:29, 40–42), though not with force. The believer is to take the punishment that might be given out by the state that would result from obedience to the higher authority of God. Although both ideas (subjection because of the Lord's example or the Christian cause) might be included in Peter's thought, the context favors the former, for this is the very line of reasoning that Peter follows in 2:22 and following.

Specifically, the believer is to be subject to the supreme human authority, to the king as supreme *(eite basilei hēs hyperechonti,* "whether to the king as supreme"). *Basileia* (king) was a common title for Caesar in the Greek-speaking part of the Roman Empire. It helps to remember that Caesar Nero was the supreme ruler of Peter's day. Caesar was considered "as supreme" *(hēs hyperechonti,* "as the supreme authority") and would be equivalent in our day to the president of the U.S., who is the supreme ruler of that country. The believer is subject to human authorities delegated by the supreme authority. These are "governors" *(hēgemosin,* proconsuls who governed the imperial and senatorial provinces), though not many countries have a parallel office appointee. In the United States the closest equivalent would be those who hold high appointed offices, such as cabinet posts, U.S. Supreme Court justices, or federal judges.

Since the supreme authority was by virtue of God's appointment, those he appoints also hold authority by virtue of God's appointment. Those in appointed authority have a twofold purpose, first, as their authority relates to evildoers and, second, as their authority relates to law-abiding citizens. They are "for the punishment of evildoers" *(eis ekdikēsin kakopoiōn)*, though *evildoers* is a relative term because it is used in reference to the state. It is the state that determines what is good and what is evil. If the state were to make a law in the spiritual realm forbidding the exercise of religion, the believer would be duty-bound to obey God rather than the government. To obey God would be good, but because the law of the state prohibits it, the state would judge the exercise of religion to be bad and would punish believers for doing "evil." In such cases, the believer is to suffer the consequences of his obedience to superior authority.

Normally, the word *evildoer (kakopoiōn)* refers only to a wicked man who does evil in such a way that he must be punished by the magistrate. The individual Christian is forbidden to usurp the law and personally avenge injuries (cf. Matt. 5:39), yet it is the duty of the state to avenge injury to the individual. Unless the state discharges its duty firmly, it cannot exist. Those in appointed authority are to keep in mind that they are "for the praise of them that do well" *(epainon de agathopoiōn)* when it comes to law-abiding citizens. Again, this is a relative determination; the parameters of what makes a citizen "law abiding" are determined by the state. What the state determines to be law-abiding behavior may run directly contrary to what God says is law abiding. The believer is to appropriate the values of the Word of God rather than society or state.

However, subjection to the state is God's will (1 Peter 2:15–17). This is specifically proclaimed, 2:15a: "For so is the will *(thelēma,* "something willed") of God." The specific thing that God wills is our subjection to the state. Here is something the believer must do to be obedient to what God specifically wills. The larger picture of God's will in this matter is explained (2:15b–16). By doing good and living in subjection, we "muzzle" *(phimoun)* the ignorance of foolish men" *(tōn aphronōn anthrōpōn agnōsian)*. It is better to prevent evil-speakers from speaking than to silence them after they have spoken. The believer, then, is to conduct his or her life so that unbelievers will not have any opportunity to speak against them. The ignorance of foolish men stems from the fact that they have not accurately observed the believers, nor have they experienced the new birth. They are totally ignorant of what is transpiring in the Christians' lives. Their judgments are wrong for they have no frame of reference with which to make proper evaluations. The foolish men are without reason. They are in want of mental sanity and have a reckless and inconsiderate habit of mind. They never stop to think that it might be they who are wrong. Instead, they conclude that they are the only ones who are right and anyone who does not conform to their standard of conduct is insane.

Our subjection to the state is a threefold subjection: (1) with "well-doing" (2:15b); (2) "as free" (2:16a); and (3) as one who uses his freedom properly (2:16b). The word *well-doing (agathopoiountas)* in this context means to subject one's self to the God-ordained authority of the state. It is not resistance (whether passive or active) that will silence the ignorance of the foolish. Subjection, a concept quite foreign to the human mind, is the manner by which it is to be done. The words *as free (eleutheroi)* set forth the believer's relationship to the state. This freedom, however, is not absolute, for the believer is God's slave. The reality is that the superior relationship of slavery to God is to govern his or her relationship to the state. As God's slave, the Christian will be subject to the state because this is God's will and Christ's example. The simple truth is that *the believer who is not subject to the state is not subject to God.* This is true even if one lives in a totalitarian state. This subjection on the part of the believer is designed to put to silence the ignorance of foolish men.

Real freedom from the state (that only the believer can experience) must not serve "for a cloak of maliciousness" *(hōs epikalymma echontes tēs kakias)*. It must not be resistance that departs from subjection to God-ordained authority. The ultimate reason for subjection to the state is the position of slavery to God. Since God is master, and the state is God's creation for the orderly discharge of human affairs, the believer is to be subject to whomever God has given jurisdiction. The believer who is not subject to the state is not subject to God. Yet, the believer must realize that this relation to the state springs from relation to God and not from any inherent obligation the state itself may claim. Christian freedom rests not on escape from service, but on a change of master.[1] The idea that Christians are both free and servants of God has always been an offense in the eyes of totalitarian political philosophy and accounts for attempts, ancient and modern, to suppress Christianity.

God's will is explained in 1 Peter 2:17 and is based on the reason set forth in 2:15–16. First Peter 2:17 gets to the heart of Peter's theology regarding the state. Peter states his application as a general principle: "Honor all men." He then shows how this general principle works in the ecclesiastical sphere: "Love the brotherhood"; "fear God"; "honor the king."

*Second, the believer is to "honor all men."* Here, Peter commands us to give others the respect and courtesy due to them as human beings. It is this general principle and obligation that is missing from totalitarian political philosophies that seek to sacrifice the essential worth of the individual to the state. It is also missing in materialistic political schools of thought that regard individuals only as "hands" or "machines" to be used to accomplish the state's wishes.

Whereas a general reverence is enjoined for all, the believer is commanded to a different commitment, "love" for fellow Christians. This is the fruit of the Spirit kind of love (cf. Gal. 5:22) and is possible only when the believer is properly in step with the Holy Spirit, with all known sins confessed. In the personal sphere, the believer is to "fear God" (cf. 1:17).

The believer's continuous attitude toward God is to be one of reverence. This reverence should temper all thought and actions and should be the motive for either doing or abstaining from doing certain things. It is important to note that this is not cringing fear before God, in which the creature is fearful of what the Creator might do at any moment. It is, rather, a fear that holds God in highest awe and reverence. In the political sphere, the believer is to honor the king. This is to be the believer's continuous attitude toward the one who has supreme human authority and delegates with that authority. It is, of course, the practical outworking of the submission enjoined in 2:13. If the believer is subject to the supreme authority, he or she will honor that authority.

## The Realms of Believer Responsibility

First Peter 2:13–3:12 clearly sets forth three realms in which the believer has responsibility. They are (1) to the state or public affairs (2:13–17), (2) to the household, or professional affairs (2:18–25), and (3) to the home, or private affairs (3:1–7). In each of these realms, the believer is to be in subjection for the Lord's sake (see 2:13). God has a specific desire concerning the believer's conduct in each of these realms, and it is the believer's responsibility to be in subjection to proper authority in each. The believer is to be in subjection to the state's God-ordained rulers. The believer is to be in subjection to the household's God-ordained master, the boss. The believer is to be in subjection in the home. God commands the wife to be subject to the husband, her God-ordained head. And God commands the husband to be subject to God in his God-ordained responsibility of headship. He must dwell together with his wife *(synoikountes)*. The idea expressed is for the husband to take his wife into every aspect of his life, rendering to her the honor due because she is his wife and fellow heir of salvation.

As long as God-ordained authority is operating according to its God-ordained responsibility in each of these realms, all is well. The believer has only one responsibility—subjection. However, confusion comes when one of these realms seeks to operate in the domain of the other. For example, if the state were to pass legislation forbidding the worship of God, the believer feels an immediate impact. God has commanded that we worship, and we are obligated to obey.

The state, however, has declared the worship of God to be evil according to its value system, and those who worship Him will be duly punished. The believer, then, is in a quandary: obey God or obey the state? The believer, however, must recognize God as the higher authority and must worship Him. Thus, even though he does good as far as God is concerned, he becomes an evildoer as far as the state is concerned and is subject to punishment. In such an instance, the believer is not to seek to resist or overthrow the state or to thwart its effort to punish. The state is operating within its God-given authority (Rom. 13:3–4). This principle is seen in the lives of the Old Testament heroes Hananiah, Mishael, and Azariah when they refused to worship Nebuchadnezzar's image (Daniel 3) and Daniel when he refused to give up praying to Yahweh (Daniel 6). In modern days, when governments have forbidden Christians to bring Bibles into a country, those who smuggle Bibles must be willing to accept the potential outcome of their actions. Any time a believer determines to undertake an action in obedience to God and that action is against the law, that person must be ready to accept the consequences without complaint.

## *Conclusion*

The proper biblical relationship between the state and the church (i.e., believers) can be summarized with six practical corollaries:

1.  The church is not to dominate the state.
2.  The state is not to dominate the church.
3.  The church is to be independent of the state.
4.  The state is to be independent of the church.
5.  The church is to give the state its value system.
6.  The state is to provide the church with protection to carry out its worship of God freely.

Only the Lord knows what this next one hundred years will bring. So many Christians around the world have never experienced freedom from government interference. Some people argue that persecution only fans the flames of evangelism and actually causes the church to grow stronger. Meanwhile, we have a mandate to pray for those in authority that we may live peacefully with all, that the gospel may have its free course to win men and women to Christ.

■ ■ ■ ■ ■ ■ ■ ■ ■ ■ ■ ■ ■ ■ ■ ■ ■ ■ ■ ■ ■ ■ ■ ■ ■ ■ ■ ■ ■ ■ ■ ■

# 6

# UNMASKING THE MANY FACES OF PLURALISM

## Gary P. Stewart

Pluralism threatens biblical integrity, according to most conservative evangelical thinkers. But some other evangelicals and most theological liberals say that pluralism holds out hope of unity in a world full of differences, a world that must have peace. To one side, it means compromise; to the other, cooperation. To one side, it is an excruciating push away from theological exclusivity; to the other, it is an encouraging push away from authoritarianism toward tolerance. To one side, it is corruption; to the other, compassion. To some, these lines are clearly drawn in the sand; to others, they may appear extreme. It is clear from the literature that pluralism will be the defining issue (in at least the North American mind) for the coming decades.[1]

As advanced transportation and communications technology make the world an even smaller place, national boundaries conjoin and cultures collide. The vast mountain ranges and great oceans that have always kept one group from knowing too much about another no longer bar either connectedness or conflict. Today, peace conferences can be conducted through teleconferencing, and war can be raged with an enemy that is positioned many miles "over the horizon." Economic, political, sociological, and religious differences among the world's cultures are more delineated and better understood. Humanity has become one huge tower of Babel, and many people are trying to pull the cultures back together again. If such unification is to happen in the midst of cultural diversity, there must be a unifying issue. Economically, we talk about a world market. Politically, we have seen the apparent collapse of communism with hope that some form of democracy will prevail. Sociologically, we provide educational exercises in multiculturalism so that differences can be learned, appreciated, and even assimilated. Religiously, at least in the West, "men and women of faith" are identifying common threads through the world's belief systems in order to create an ecumenical and soteriological underpinning for unity, so that no one's faith is offensive to anyone else, and religion becomes inclusive of all who *sincerely seek God.*

Pluralism is the philosophical construct that is energizing this drive for unity. We live with a plurality of views and lifestyles that both intrigues and threatens us. The dress, song, architecture, and history of others intrigue us, while we are threatened by ideologies these societies bring to our understanding of the world.

Pluralism describes the situation in which a society or world is marked by a diversity of views and outlooks. Greatly differing moral, religious, and political philosophies and ways of life compete. This creates a smorgasbord of competing and frequently incompatible views from which to choose.[2]

Can a world exist with the competition of such divergent views upon the world stage, or must all views go through a process of ecumenical collaboration that diminishes distinction for mutual inclusiveness? It is the assertion here that distinctions are important and that pluralism, which is a positive empirical indicator of these distinctions, is lost when ecumenical collaboration runs amuck. Philosophical and religious distinctions separate truth from error, and the evangelical world is in no position to embrace a philosophy that suppresses or denies the reality of absolute or biblical truth. The diversity of the world's religions exposes the light of the world more clearly. Where darkness has become a dim gray, light penetrates poorly and appears to be indistinct.

*Pluralism is an acceptable evidence of disunity* because it is the natural product of a world that seeks after God and truth with the tools of human reason. Ecumenism is an unacceptable evidence of attempted unity that blurs distinctions that are essential to unity. Biblical Christianity is an *acceptable evidence of unity* because it is the divinely ordained channel through which peace ultimately will come to the world—a world that will readily accept racial plurality. Only in the eternal kingdom of God in Christ will there be no dearth of light in which darkness can prevail. I fully realize that this view is both unacceptable to some evangelicals and thoroughly authoritarian and exclusive to a liberal view of theology, but it is my hope to persuade folks of the importance of the biblical message for future generations. My primary objective is to encourage evangelicals to resist the temptation to forego biblical distinctions for the sake of a unity that is, at best, a peripheral, temporal, earthly peace.

This chapter will focus on terms that give meaning and purpose to the reality we call pluralism. Along with the identification of each term, I will examine its impact on society and evaluate its benefits or problems.

## Terminology

This discussion is not intended to be exhaustive in gathering terms that accompany the concept of pluralism. The following words do relate, however, to the major ideas that shape the controversy. One will immediately notice that the word *pluralism* is used more descriptively but less broadly than is customary. Other terms to be discussed are *autonomy, exclusivism* and *inclusivism, multiculturalism, religious pluralism,* and *tolerance.*

### Pluralism

The word *pluralism* has come to be so broadly used over the years that we feel compelled to bring it back to its clear and accurate meaning. What writers generally refer to as pluralism is understood here as religious or political *tolerance, diversity,* and *ecumenism.*[3] Properly, pluralism identifies the reality of differing races, languages, values, religions, and ideologies within a given society or within the global perspective. Pluralism keeps in view what these societal differences are and are not and how they interrelate. It deals with one social group's feelings of superiority over another. Pluralism has been a fact of life since the tower of Babel. What is different about pluralism in the modern world is that different societies now encounter each other so frequently. In ancient history, cultures remained more or less isolated, except for the occasional war that subjugated peoples and their cultures to the rule of the occupying force. Pluralism was present in the world, but tolerance of differences and concern for national autonomy was not regarded as a redeeming human quality. Today, we have near instantaneous national and international access to differing cultures and their views. In the United States and Europe, immigration has permitted people of various nationalities and religious persuasions to flourish side by side. *Descriptive pluralism*—or *empirical pluralism* as D. A. Carson refers to it—describes the presence of people from differing cultures and perspectives.[4] Pluralism understands that different animals live in different cages in the zoo.

What happens when pluralism has no national boundary? In

the twentieth century, pluralism could no longer be viewed simply as personal awareness of the world situation. Now it was universal personal experience. Potentially, national or global pluralism leads to a cultural paradox: The pain of partisanship among unique cultures in near proximity begs for unanimity. Unanimity erodes uniqueness. How can a society be both pluralistic and unified? This is the primary struggle that pluralism brings to modern politicians and theologians alike.

The challenge associated with pluralism and the theologies of the various religions that comprise a society is to discern how to coexist without sacrificing distinctives for the sake of unanimity. The evangelical must accept that in a fallen world, genuine and complete unanimity is incompatible with, though tolerant of, pluralism. The theology of biblical Christianity provides more than adequate instruction to help evangelicals live at peace in a pluralistic world.

## Multiculturalism

*Multiculturalism* comes as a response to "pluralism without borders." As various cultures develop together within a nation, the responsibility to incorporate each culture's views, traditions, and talents into the mainstream of society is essential to justice and peace. *Multiculturalism strives for unity within a pluralistic setting.* To use our previous analogy, multiculturalism realizes that there are many different animals in the zoo but recognizes that they must learn to live together in one cage. A multicultural society seeks to include all of its cultural resources in developing its religious, political, legal, artistic, and family institutions. It considers the ideas and concerns of men and women of all sizes, shapes, races, and religions to address the larger picture with a more complete understanding of reality. Justice implies that all sides have a voice in the forum and that their views carry equal weight. Since each person tends to feel cheated or slighted when personal opinions are not honored, there must be an overriding instrument of discernment, acceptable to all, that adjudicates matters fairly. In the United States, for example, this instrument has been the U.S. Constitution.

For about the first 180 years, the Constitution was interpreted from a relatively consistent Christian moral perspective. But with the rise of postmodernism and its theory that all truth is relative (so no one truth is more valid than another), the Constitution was slowly eroded into a relativistic document that could be interpreted at a lawyer's, or a judge's, discretion. With truth being relative, the courts are now obligated to address the opinions of any and all

interest groups that claim to be discriminated against. Accommo-
dation, sensitivity, inclusion, cooperation, and harmony have become ends that are reached without any moral consideration or
consensus. Even virtues common to most religions are ignored in
the name of sensitivity. Multiculturalism has been skewed toward a
secular understanding of the world. Although multiculturalism is
not the ultimate answer, as a concept its respect for all of humanity
is commendable. But without a moral underpinning, it becomes
divisive and perpetuates disorder. Multiculturalism also carries
much baggage that ought to worry Christians. This baggage has
less to do with the details of multiculturalism than with its general
orientation. Notice that those who favor multiculturalism do not
argue on the basis of a desire for justice. Rather, multiculturalism's
practical necessity becomes the ultimate good.[5]

Multiculturalism is no longer simply an attempt to conjoin various cultures within a society. It is becoming a worldview in its own
right, a totally secular one. It is a culture within a culture, a worldview
of amalgamated conflicting worldviews. It attempts to join people
for the sake of political and commercial benefit, rather than for
reasons of truth and justice. Where there is no absolute truth, people
have nothing left but a smorgasbord of equally valid ideas. This
removes the shackles of morality, but ultimately ends in social chaos.
This drives religious groups and cultures back to the comforts of
their distinctiveness. Multiculturalism has created a pragmatic culture that is distinct from, yet inclusive of, other cultures. People
actually live in two cultures, one in which they work and one in
which they live at home. However, multiculturalism's appreciation
and encouragement of differences in a context of relativity has
gradually pushed the United States away from national unity into
a form of tribalism. It has promoted the extreme division with which
Canadians now struggle. It has promoted a consolidation of cultures into geographical areas, and therefore solidarity of purpose
apart from other cultures. In Europe and North America, this has
been used to stir hatred among fringe groups from neo-Nazis to
skinheads who promote ethnic or racial purity. Radical feminists
and "gay rights" groups make much of these arguments.

This is already clearly depicted on North America's university
campuses where the experiment of secular multiculturalism has
existed for over a generation.

> Eager to accommodate all oppressed minorities, many
> college campuses today segment them all the more. After
> all the hard-fought battles to integrate higher education,

today we see a re-segregation of the university. Racial
minorities often have separate dormitories, separate
dining areas, separate student unions, separate yearbooks,
and separate graduation ceremonies. Affirmative action
programs base admissions and scholarships on race,
unfairly stigmatizing qualified minority students by
implying that they could not succeed on their merits
alone. Though all this multiculturalism aims at promoting tolerance, more racial tension and animosity exists
on campuses today than ever.[6]

Samuel P. Huntington, in a recent article in *Foreign Affairs*,
remarking on multiculturalism and immigration in the United
States (and applicable to Canada as well), observed:

Until recently immigrant groups came to America because they saw immigration as an opportunity to become
American. To what extent now, however, do people come
because they see it as an opportunity to remain themselves? Previously immigrants felt discriminated against
if they were not permitted to join the mainstream. Now
it appears that some groups feel discriminated against if
they are not allowed to remain apart from the mainstream.

The ideologies of multiculturalism and diversity rein-
force and legitimate these trends. They deny the existence of a common culture in the United States, denounce
assimilation, and promote the primacy of racial, ethnic,
and other subnational cultural identities and groupings.
They also question a central element in the American
Creed by substituting for the rights of individuals the
rights of groups, defined largely in terms of race,
ethnicity, gender, and sexual preference.[7]

Multiculturalism's relativistic roots have focused so much on
accommodating and tolerating distinctions that it has overlooked
similarities. The result is a society full of distinctly independent
cultural groups, each demanding the right to live according to its
own dictates.

Along these lines, it is interesting to note Huntington's prognosis.
People tend to draw their identity from ancestry, religion, language,
history, values, customs, and institutions. They identify with
cultural groups: tribes; ethnic groups; religious communities; nations;

and most broadly speaking, civilizations.[8] Huntington's civilizational model identifies eight distinct civilizations: Islamic; Sinic (centered on the "core state" of China); Western; Orthodox (centered on Russia); Japanese; Hindu; Latin American; and African. Africa's wide cultural and political differences make this category somewhat tentative. Of these eight, geopolitically, Huntington believes the great twenty-first-century clashes and struggles will be among Islam, the West, and China. The conflicts among these cultures will arise, in part, due to "Western arrogance, Islamic intolerance, and Sinic assertiveness."[9] Some cultural distinctions are dangerous. The attitudes and policies of some civilizations are incompatible with pluralism and intolerant of pluralism. A multiculturalism that genuinely seeks uniformity amidst a plurality must never lose sight of humanity's more sinister side.

One particular cultural group where this is abundantly true is Islam. Where Islam becomes dominant, it negates cultural differences by applying Shari'a (Islamic law) to the non-Muslim population. According to Nina Shea:

> The militant Islamic government's tactics in its religious war in the southern part of the country [Sudan near the end of the twentieth century] have resulted in the deaths of about 1.5 million people and the displacement of more than 3 million. Sudanese agents burned and looted villages, enslaved women and children, forcibly converted non-Muslim boys before using them as shock troops in battle, relocated entire villages into concentration camps called "peace villages," and withheld international food aid to non-Muslim communities.[10]

Multiculturalism cannot work where people ascribe to doctrines that demean and subjugate those who hold "heretical" positions. Over the twentieth century, the Christian presence in Iraq dwindled from 35 percent to 5 percent of the population, in Iran from 15 percent to 2 percent, in Syria from 40 percent to 10 percent, and in Turkey from 32 percent to 0.2 percent. Christians have good reason to be concerned with the eradication of the Christian perspective from the public square. Christians are the most persecuted religious group on earth today,[11] and multiculturalism as a secular system does not offer much hope of bringing greater acceptance. The reality of Islamic persecution in Sudan is grim evidence of the ideological threat. "The underlying problem for the West is not Islamic fundamentalism. It is Islam, a different civilization whose people are convinced of the superiority of their culture and are obsessed with the inferiority of their power," Huntington declares.[12]

The answer would be a national or international order that appreciates cultural distinctions but defines them in the context of truth, justice, and morality. Each culture must give up some of its distinctions for the sake of peace with others. What is practiced fully in the mosque, synagogue, temple, and church must be moderated in the public square. We must find the principles and absolutes that are common among cultures. Gene Veith correctly admonishes schools to study cultures more deeply, to get beneath the surface. If they would do so, "it would be evident that cultures do not all think differently. Actually there is a great deal of cross-cultural agreement, especially in areas unfashionable to postmodernists, such as moral responsibility."[13] Every culture understands that human nature needs to be "caged" by some moral absolutes to avoid having people running loose on society like a herd of animals.

### Tolerance

When one hears the word *tolerance*, mental and emotional reactions immediately begin to surface. What is actually meant by the word is left to each individual's philosophical perspective on life and truth. Those from a more traditional background tend to view tolerance as a questionable virtue that undermines and diminishes their orthodox belief in the transcendent. Those who espouse progressivism view tolerance as an opportunity to pursue a personal and autonomous agenda without interference. To the traditionalist, tolerance is a threat to morality and objective truth; to the progressivist, it is a key that unlocks the shackles of moral restraint and intellectual narrowness.

How are Christians to react to this "politically correct" virtue? Stan D. Gaede advises believers to respond to the secular view of tolerance from a theological basis—God operates from a foundation of truth and justice and demands that those who follow Him act justly, love mercy, and walk humbly before Him (Mic. 6:8).[14] We are His representatives to a world that is confused about truth and, therefore, is incapable of exacting justice equitably. Global pluralism has produced an unstable multicultural diversity. This diversity becomes a government mandate as a standard for politically correct behavior. Implicit is a denial of absolute, objective truth. It is assumed that what remains is a tolerance that asks all peoples, from all faiths and cultures, to accept all other views as equally valid.

Without any fanatic belief in absolutes, the world can have peace and security. This view of tolerance can work only if all people refrain from imposing their personal morals and beliefs on others. Boundaries of cultural and subcultural influence need to be established, not with walls, but with tolerance so that autonomous choices are not infringed upon. People must be careful not to "do or say anything that any racial, gender, cultural or sexual orientation group might find offensive." In this context, tolerance is defined as acceptance or neutrality, the evolution of a new moral standard.[15]

People have forgotten that genuine tolerance is dependent on a predefined standard. Tolerance is extended to people who, because of personal or cultural ignorance, are unaware of all that a preexisting standard requires of them. For this reason, emotional and intellectual growth is expected within a broad, but limited, time frame. At the end of this period of relaxed rules, tolerance is gradually replaced by discipline, ranging from slight to harsh according to the extent of the discrepancy. To ignore or not expect personal growth and to remain silent about a behavior that is detrimental to the community's welfare confuses tolerance with timidity. A society must have a moral standard around which tolerance operates, truth is honored, and justice prevails.

The Christian tolerance of those who live outside of evangelical faith is appropriate and understandable. Though we do not accept much of their behavior and often must make our sentiments known, we understand the theological blindness (2 Cor. 4:2–4; cf. Rom. 1:21, 28) from which their worldview originates. Therefore, we treat them compassionately and mercifully, leaving their ultimate fate in the hands of God. This is genuine tolerance; however, when tolerance is not framed within accepted moral standards, concepts such as grace, mercy, unconditional love, and forgiveness lose their meaning. Don Eberly notes that:

> to love unconditionally and forgive is not to be confused with tolerance, a term that can imply moral neutrality and consent. The spirit of forgiveness accepts others while rejecting their conduct or convictions. Few terms are more loaded with self-deception and distortion than the contemporary concept of tolerance. The growing calls for Americans to be more tolerant have not produced citizens who act with genuine benevolence toward one another.[16]

In the late 1990s, this lack of benevolence in the United States was demonstrated by political and moral upheavals that resulted when the President was found to have committed blatant sexual indiscretions. Requests to forgive the president's moral impropriety or to show mercy because of a human weakness common to us all did not appeal for genuine tolerance. Rather, the final declaration of innocence in the impeachment trial in the U.S. Senate became a mandate for determining personal and private behavior to be off-limits to public and judicial scrutiny. In the name of tolerance, the decision eliminated standards for morality and decency. Tolerance may delay justice as an expression of mercy in hopes of producing genuine repentance or change in behavior, but it never turns a blind eye to injustice or rolls over to allow adjustment of a transcendent moral standard.

As the world becomes more interconnected, there is a need for people to be tolerant of one another. But at what expense to moral standards will this toleration be purchased? We must be aware that tolerance is not an isolated phenomenon. Tolerance we might consider important and needed (racial equality, for example) frequently is expanded to areas that may seem dangerous, such as ideological tolerance of communists or atheists, or disastrous to social morality, such as tolerance for sexual perversions or cohabiting outside of marriage.[17]

Sensitivity in a multicultural world addresses issues that demand change. Prejudice and discrimination against people because of race, place of birth, or gender is intolerable, and we should be sensitive to the customs and struggles of all peoples. But tolerance and sensitivity are not ends in themselves. They are virtues that govern interaction but never at the expense of truth and justice. Behaviors are not wrong because they are insensitive; they are wrong because an objective truth declares that they are unjust. It is also true that, in a smaller world, international trade demands tolerance for economic growth. But to seek financial security at the expense of truth and justice opens the door to passively giving a "stamp of approval" or turning a blind eye to a trading partner's internal human-rights violations for the sake of business or a profit.

The West has moved toward "indiscriminate inclusion" apart from a moral foundation. Everything is accepted, so nothing can be identified as right. "And so we deny the need for such a foundation of rightness and hope against hope that we can build a decent society undergirded by relativism," writes Gaede. "For that reason we promote multiculturalism—not as an effort to establish justice based on some moral vision, but simply to achieve indiscriminate inclusion. But what we end up with is not tolerance, nor inclusion, and certainly not justice." What we get, Gaede warns, is a moral vacuum into which a despot such as Robespierre stepped in the French Revolution. People with power decide what is "best" for all and execute their will accordingly.[18]

In a world of unbridled tolerance, someone will have ultimate power to press his or her will. If that someone has a philosophy that is anti-Christian, his or her tolerance will be selective. Believers must be people of conviction who take responsibility for what they know and share it, rather than look at their knowledge as an achievement that deserves respect. We forget the power that is inherent in the gospel and its ability to thwart the powers of evil. In a commentary on politically correct philosophy, Gaede observed the Christian ideal that "we are inclusive of people but not of beliefs. We ought to listen and learn from all people, but we will not agree with all people. We will embrace the speaker but not the spoken lie."[19]

We who deserve death are spared that fate by the love of One who was willing to die for us. Christ's sacrificial act must be offered to others through lives that reflect understanding, humility, and peace, but never at the expense of truth and justice. Jesus loved everyone despite race, class, or creed (the Roman centurion, the Samaritan woman, the blind, and the poor), but His love was genuine, and, therefore, did not overlook false witness and injustice. He "imposed" His character and the will of His Father upon the society of His time and it cost Him His life. Are we unwilling to live up to the standard He designed for us? Are we to run from suffering under the pretense of a human philosophy that suggests that tolerance, and not a transcendent God, is the way to peace? I think not.

The modern world does not know how to deal with the issue of differences. It doesn't have the categories to do so. And so it vacillates between a blind affirmation of differences and an equally blind affirmation of similarities, looking to politics of inclusion or exclusion to save us. But they will not save us. Only Jesus saves. And it is only as we take our cue from Him and build our policies on the truth that He has given us that we will be able to serve a very needy world.[20]

James Hunter accurately describes a valid multicultural playing field in his suggestion that a "principled tolerance is what common life in contemporary America is all about. But this is only possible if all contenders, however much they disagree with each other on principle, do not kill each other over these differences, do not desecrate what the other holds sublime, and do not eschew principled discourse with the other."[21]

## Autonomy

The desire to be free is as old as the fall of Adam and Eve. From that time to the present, humanity has sought tenaciously to create its own sovereignty as nations and as individuals. The issue of our time, of any time, is anthropological; what is to be done with the self and how much control over the self can, or should, one have? Does autonomy provide the answer to this problem, or does it lead to confusion, deception, and obscurity?

The philosophical debate over autonomy throughout this century has led to the atrocity of the holocaust, the legalization in the United States of abortion in 1973 and other nations through the same period, and epidemic physician-assisted suicide in Scandinavia and increasingly in the United States. The concept of autonomy is debated because scholars are not blind to its obvious shortcomings, especially in the broad area of medicine. James Childress and John Fletcher write in an essay on medical ethics and personal autonomy that, while biomedical ethics believes a central consideration must be given to the principle of respect for autonomy, the demands of autonomy are often unclear. Personal actions and values are complex, and autonomy cannot be the only source of moral guidance.[22] The respect of personal autonomy is "individualized and context-related. [Scholars] maintain that the autonomous human being is to some extent self-determining but limited by other's autonomy and perhaps further moral constraints."[23] The word *autonomy* is too direct or determinative to satisfy the moral care of the individual and the moral responsibility that individual has toward others. Thomas Murray correctly reminds us of the paternalistic treatment patients received from health care professionals and of how important it is:

> to stand up and protest. Autonomy was a powerful and handy concept with which to do that. Because it touched such deep currents in American character and culture, autonomy cast a dazzling glow that many hoped would be able to illuminate all the dark corners of our shared moral life. Some still retain that faith; others, such as myself, believe that autonomy remains a vital moral bulwark against oppression, but that it is not an all-encompassing guide to living good lives or building good communities.[24]

Though I agree with Murray about the disrespectful abuses of the individual by paternalistic medicine and that autonomy is not a "guide to living good lives," I believe that arguing from the perspective of self-rule or autonomy is misleading and ill-advised. The term is overly pregnant with meaning and cannot adequately provide balance to the issue of paternalism. It is simply too self-enhancing and contradicts the reality and presence of numerous external influences to be of lasting and meaningful value. Additionally, E. D. Cook affirms that "autonomy is always limited in a society. People are not free to do whatever they want with their own bodies, as legislation on seat belts, motorcycle helmets, prostitution, surrogacy and pornography indicates. Autonomy is limited, where the best interests of another are at stake. This may be a part of the proper exercise of a professional responsibility."[25]

Gilbert Meilaender concurs by arguing that it is unrealistic to suggest that individuals are constructed apart from their environments; these he delineates as the family, the determinative world of nature, significant relationships, and God. It is in one's relationship with God that one's true value is determined, a fact that "requires that we abandon the ideal of the autonomous person."[26] Another way of looking at individuals in relation to their environment must be sought, one that prevents injustice and is consistent with the biblical record.

It appears to me that relativism is a logical extension of autonomy. Relativism claims that there is no truth or that truth is personally or culturally determined. To rule oneself (autonomy) demands that one decides for oneself (relativism), which leads to self-divination or self-destruction. From recent studies, it appears that relativism, and therefore personal autonomy, is prevalent. One study examined the North American mentality of making the moral rules to fit the circumstance. Thirteen percent of those questioned expressed approval for all of the Ten Commandments. Forty percent were willing to accept five of the ten. No wonder the moral consensus that held as recently as the 1950s has shattered. There is little respect for institutions or law. Personal autonomy rules over any other authority. In the same survey, 93 percent of those surveyed declared that they alone determine what is moral in their lives. They base their decisions on their experiences or on whims. Almost as large a majority (84 percent) confessed that they would violate the established rules of their religion if they thought it was wrong. Eighty-one percent said that they had done so.[27]

The soil, in which the roots of libertarianism[28] can grow deeply, is becoming more fertile each day. Pluralism, multiculturalism, and diversity have developed alongside autonomy and relativism to diminish the authority and power that accompany truth. Individual rights and personal opinion without outside authority dismantles unity, segregates, and leads ultimately to hostility. From a practical point of view, humanity's concern for survival may be the one mitigating factor that prevents autonomy from becoming absolute and chaotic. From a theological point of view, autonomy is subordinate to the sovereign design of the Lord and can progress only within the limits of His plan.

Autonomy in a multicultural setting jettisons external constraints in favor of internal desires. However, there is one external guide and constraint that must be an integral part of every culture. It is an influence that fools resist but to which the wise person clings. It is the Word of God (Prov. 1:7; 12:1; 13:18). Instruction and reproof come from God and are attended to by the wise but hated by the "stupid" in society (12:1). One imperative from Scripture makes life by autonomy (self-rule) impossible. This instruction from God declares an antithesis to society's understanding of autonomy.

Believers are told to "love your neighbor as yourself" (Lev. 19:18; Matt. 19:19, 22:39; Mark. 12:31; Rom. 13:9; Gal. 5:14; and James 2:8). They are to be "devoted to one another in brotherly love." We are to "give preference to one another in honor" (Rom. 12:10). It is interesting that the Bible does not, in fact, instruct us to love ourselves. Loving ourselves is natural (Eph. 5:29) and, therefore, does not need to be commanded. In fact, it is so natural that in our fallen state, loving ourselves is our major problem; hence, the numerous admonitions in Scripture to love others and prefer them to ourselves. Autonomy, which arises from self-love and a longing for control, is the natural principle of dominion for a fallen people. It takes us away from the authority of God, of governments (see Rom. 13:1–4, which demands submission of people to governments), of employers, and of educators to pursue our own ends. At its core, it is isolating and self-destructive, as the physician-assisted suicide debate reveals. H. Wayne House admonishes believers to consider that "until we recognize our addiction to self-love as a self-centered orientation to life, we will be spiritual, as well as social, cripples. We must disavow the secular orientation we have learned so well from the world. We need to freely admit that we already love ourselves, thrive on attention, and would rather talk about ourselves than anyone else in the world."[29]

The more autonomous we become, the less concerned we become with community issues that don't directly involve us. Autonomous individuals do what serves themselves in order to feel right; spiritual individuals do what serves God and others in order to be right. Autonomous individuals make decisions that satisfy themselves; spiritual individuals make decisions to satisfy God. Community cannot be enhanced by individuals who have as their first and possibly only priority their own agenda and welfare. Consider a Christian woman who prepares an advanced directive that requests life-sustaining measures "at all costs." Her thoughts about her own existence and survival do not take into account the effect her directive will have on her family, the health care professionals who must tend to her day after day, or the resources that will be wasted in prolonging a life that would have naturally succumbed to the disease weeks earlier. Her autonomous will has left a testimony inconsistent with a mature faith in God.

Our life-and-death decisions must always take into account the impact they will have on others. Paul admonishes us to do "nothing from selfishness or empty conceit, but with humility of mind let each of you regard one another as more important than himself; do not merely look out for your own personal interests, but also for the interests of others" (Phil. 2:3–4). Autonomy, by definition, does not allow the individual to consider the needs of others before his or her own and is, therefore, inconsistent with the biblical record. Willard Gaylin's assessment that "there cannot be a moral creature without autonomy and choice" is only partially correct.[30] It should be clear from the Genesis account that acting out in autonomous fashion places the individual with free will in conflict with the Creator.

The philosophical confusion over autonomy is perpetuated because philosophers insist on pursuing a principle of freedom (autonomy) that is inconsistent with good order and discipline (i.e., external guidance from God). It is interesting to note that even philosophers recognize the chaotic consequences of a consistent autonomy and, therefore, struggle unsuccessfully to explain how individuality, community, and responsibility fit together into the concept. "Where is the wise man? Where is the scribe? Where is the debater of this age? Has not God made foolish the wisdom of the world?" (1 Cor. 1:20).

Without an acceptance of God, one will always be enticed to control one's own life and live independently of external authorities. The concept of autonomy is natural where no unifying authority exists or where a despotic authority rules. Daniel Callahan is right regarding his concern that bioethics "pursue with sufficient imagination the idea of the common good, or public interest, on the one hand, and that of personal responsibility, or the moral uses of individual choice, on the other."[31] A respect for autonomy is inherently incompatible with communal good and responsible individuality, whereas respect for the individual protects individuals from abuse in that it focuses each individual's attention on the welfare of other individuals. Good moral choices are more likely to occur in a society whose members look out primarily for one another rather than independently of one another for personal benefit. No decision that we make should be made independently of the impact it might have on the community at large. Christians have an authority that entreats us to prefer the interests of others above our own and to treat others the way we would want to be treated. Respect for an individual has nothing whatsoever to do with autonomy; it has everything to do with the fact that each individual has received innate value simply by being made in the image of God. The sacrifices that come to us when we choose "never to pay back evil for evil to anyone," to "respect what is right in the sight of all men," and "if possible, so far as it depends on you" to "be at peace with all men" (Rom. 12:17–18) will ultimately bring greater peace and freedom to each individual and their communities. Without God's instruction, we will not gain a genuine respect for one another.

## Religious Pluralism

The position of the orthodox church historically can be called *exclusivism*. No one comes to the Father except through faith in Jesus. All other paths to God are excluded as unable to save. As Christians have become more acquainted with world religions, however, some of them have been impressed by the commitment people from other faiths have to seek and know their god. This, coupled with human compassion for the lost and an overemphasis on the immanent nature of God, has caused some scholars to rethink Christian doctrines of salvation and damnation. One often hears that such sincerity of faith cannot go unnoticed by a compassionate and gracious God. As a result, two new theological theories have been posited over the years: *religious pluralism* (also called universalism) and *inclusivism*.

Religious pluralism is confusing. At first glance, it appears to simply refer to a multiplicity of differing religions; however, it is more than that. From its most prominent proponent, we are able to understand its tenets and goals. Ultimately, it is a multireligious and universal approach to salvation. John Hick contends that all theology is a human creation that does not accurately reflect the heart and will of the "Ultimate Reality." In fact, each religion represents a human attempt to describe the Ultimate Reality. Therefore, each is of equal value. Hick believes his theology describes the reality of world religion:

God is known in the synagogues as Adonai, the Lord
God of Abraham, Isaac, and Jacob; in the mosques as
Allah rahmin rahim, God beneficent and merciful; in
the Sikh gurudwaras as God, who is Father, Lover,
Master, and the Great Giver, referred to as war guru;
and in the Hindu temples as Vishnu, Krishna (an incar-
nation of Vishnu), Rama, Shiva, and many other gods
and goddesses, all of whom, however, are seen as mani-
festations of the ultimate reality of Brahman; and in the
Christian churches as the triune God, Father, Son, and
Holy Spirit. And yet all these communities agree that
there can ultimately be only one God![32]

Having dismissed the value of Christian Scriptures, Hick is free
to create any theology of his pleasing to satisfy his personal understanding of God. In fact, no Scripture from any faith can convince
Hick of a theological position, since all are of human origination.
It is the position of the religious pluralist that sincerity of faith is
the ground for acceptance by the "Real." Hick compares the morality of non-Christians with that of Christians and concludes that
there is no visible difference. Therefore, non-Christian religions
are experiencing the same "fruits of the Spirit" Christians do. Their
desire to seek out God has produced a morality that is evidence of
their salvation. Hick proposes that we:

> think of salvation in more universal terms than has been
> customary in Christian theology. This in turn leads to a
> new understanding of the functions of world religions,
> including Christianity. If we define salvation as being
> forgiven and accepted by God because of Jesus' death
> on the cross, then it becomes a tautology that Christian-
> ity alone knows and is able to preach the source of salva-
> tion. But if we define salvation as an actual human
> change, a gradual transformation from natural self-
> centeredness (with all the human evils that flow from
> this) to a radically new orientation centered in God and
> manifested in the "fruit of the Spirit," then it seems clear
> that salvation is taking place within all world religions.[33]

If Christians can accept the fact that God has never accurately
revealed Himself in any particular way or to any particular people,
then any means of acquiring salvation, including Hick's, is open
for consideration. If personal experience, observation, and a "cosmic

optimism" is all that is required, and if salvation is ultimately universal, as Hick states, then I must confess that the Real is the most brutal of gods to delay ending what is nothing more than a history of senseless human tragedy.[34] To love a god of my own creation, whether I am a Christian or a Buddhist, is to commit to a contrived reality that is nothing more than the figment of human imagination. I might as well create a religion that satisfies more of my human desires and requires fewer risks, and then, be sure to follow it with great sincerity. As long as my morals are somewhat consistent with that of other people's attempts to know the Real, I'll be fine; in fact, from a universalist perspective, all will work out well anyway.

Religious pluralism—or universalism—is a postmodern position that promotes diversity without unity and relativism without absolutes. Like most postmodern philosophies, universalism accepts contradiction as normative and is therefore intellectually deceitful and irresponsible.[35] A "radical hermeneutic" dismisses objective truth in order to place the world of politics and religion on an equal footing. To avoid superiority of one group over another, the salvific plan of God in Christ is reduced to a socially constructed sincere attempt to find God.[36] One wonders if a universalist considers universalism superior to other religions or whether members of other religions are willing to submit to the superiority of Western universalism. On both counts, I doubt it![37]

## Inclusivism and Exclusivism

The debate in evangelicalism does not involve universalism. Since the late 1980s, evangelicals have pondered over at least two questions regarding the salvation of the untold: Is Jesus Christ the only path to salvation? Must one place faith in Jesus Christ as Savior to receive eternal life?[38] The first is the ontological argument that salvation is in Christ; the second is the epistemological argument that salvation comes to those who know Christ. Inclusivists suggest lenience for those who have not heard the gospel. While maintaining that salvation is ontological (only through Jesus), they do not affirm that salvation is also epistemological (to be saved, one must know or place their faith in the person of Jesus Christ). They answer yes to the first question and no to the second. Inclusivists are not universalists for they believe that those who actually hear the gospel and reject it will be lost; however, "those who have never heard might come to the Father through the Son even though they may not know much about the atonement."[39]

Clark Pinnock argues that the grace of God is at work throughout the world in the person of the Holy Spirit "in the context of non-Christian religions. Inclusivism runs a risk of suspicion in the suggestion that non-Christian religions may be not only the means of a natural knowledge of God, but also the locale of God's grace given to the world because of Christ."[40] General or natural revelation is as salvific a force as specific revelation. With the help of the omnipresent Spirit of God, salvation is through Christ, but it does not require knowledge of the Savior. It is interesting to note that the initial motivation for the inclusive position, and that of the universalist, is emotional. John B. Cobb, Jr., declares:

> I object to exclusivism because it consigns all those who do not have faith in Jesus Christ to perdition, however that perdition is understood. This simply does not fit with our experience of the spiritual stature of many faithful Jews, Hindus, Buddhists, and Muslims. The God we know in Jesus Christ cannot be thought to condemn those who display such manifest sanctity simply because they reject our Christian theology and refuse to become Protestant, Catholic, or Orthodox.[41]

As theologians continue to lean on their own understanding (Prov. 3:5–6) rather than rely on the incomprehensible knowledge of God regarding such difficult matters, they will continue to found theologies based on the wisdom of humans. We must also not fall prey to the belief that a fear of "God" is equal to salvation in Christ. The demons tremble at God, yet have no faith (James 2:19). Cornelius was a devout man who feared God, yet he did not become a Christian until he believed in Jesus, through whom he received forgiveness (Acts 10:2, 43–48). And it is clear that the apostle Paul taught that "zeal for God" is useless when it does not originate from a knowledge of the righteousness of Christ (Rom. 10:2–10). Salvation is more than fear and good works (Eph. 2:8–9). The concept of "eternal injustice" is so profound among inclusivists that they have suggested that the Scriptures teach postmortem redemption as a last chance offer (1 Peter 3:18–22) and annihilation for those who, in complete awareness of the truth, persist in rebellion against God (Phil. 3:19; 1 Thess. 5:2; 2 Thess. 1:9; 2 Peter 3:7).[42] The grisly reality of the eternal condemnation of the wicked is too much to bear in light of a God who is loving and merciful. Genuine Christians feel heartfelt sorrow about the condemnation of the lost (Luke 19:41–44; 23:28–31; and Rom. 9:2–3). The reality of hell brings joy to no one. Yet it is vividly described, along with why it is necessary, in Scripture. Jude gives a metaphorical description of hell as a "black darkness," clearly stating that the experience is forever.

The idea that Christ exists in all religions in some anonymous way is inconsistent with the message of the Old and New Testaments. Carl F. H. Henry echoes this sentiment:

> The notion that God's historical covenants embrace all world religions within the church is alien to biblical teaching. So is the teaching that Christ is present in nonbiblical religious history arbitrarily and that he correlates religion in general with redemption. The New Testament does indeed represent the whole cosmos and all history as finding its final reconciliation in Christ. But from this emphasis we cannot logically infer that nonbiblical religious writings point to Christ in some hidden way. While God's saving design in the Bible has certain universal implications, it does not welcome the world's works-religions as prefatory to the propitiatory work of the Redeemer.[43]

On the other hand, exclusivists maintain a limited view of salvation, holding that salvation is in Christ and that knowledge of Him is essential to avoid damnation. To both questions asked above, they would answer yes—salvation is found only in Jesus Christ through faith.

Normally, it is also held that salvation cannot be attained through the structure or claims of other religions. It does not hold that every other religion is wrong in every respect. Nor does it claim that all who claim to be Christians are saved or right in every respect. It does insist that where other religions are contradicted by the gracious self-disclosure of Christ, they must necessarily be wrong.[44]

Exclusivists seek to stay true to the intent of Scripture rather than find ways to reinterpret or dismiss the text through deconstructionist methods.[45] The apostle Paul reminds us that "there is none righteous, no, not one; there is none who understands; there is none who seeks after God" (Rom. 3:10–11 NKJV). The suggestion that people in all cultures and countries are genuinely seeking after the one true God, or that they are able to find Him in any religion, is inconsistent with the biblical record. Also, Hick's belief that morality is synonymous with righteousness is simply inconsistent with human experience.

My life before Christ came into my heart was as moral as that of any Christian, Muslim, Buddhist, or Hindu I have ever known. But my righteousness was my own and not Christ's. I believed in God, but I did not know that I needed the righteousness of Christ until I heard the gospel message. The Lord had drawn me to a place where I could hear and respond to the gospel and receive the righteousness of Christ. Now I strive to live a moral life to honor Him for what He has done for me, not from fear of parental discipline and disappointment or because of a personal preference. Morality, styles of worship, religious spirituality, and commitment to one's beliefs occur in people's lives for many reasons, both good and bad. To suggest that they are evidences of salvation in those who have not heard or who practice a non-Christian faith gives salvific quality to these traits that is not supported biblically. If human righteousness was an evidence of salvation, why would Christ have treated the "righteous" Pharisees with such contempt and disdain (Matt. 23:13–36)? The Scriptures are clear that only in Christ and His imputed righteousness can we receive salvation from God (Luke 24:47; John 1:12; 3:16–18; 14:6; 17:20; Acts 4:12; 26:15–18; Rom. 5:1; 6:23; 10:1–15; 2 Cor. 5:18–21; Eph. 1:7; 2:8–9; Phil. 2:5–11; Col. 1:9–14; 1 Tim. 2:4–5; Heb. 1:2–4; 1 Peter 1:17–21).

It grieves me deeply to think of the suffering that awaits those who reject or do not hear the Good News (see Luke 16:19–26), among them friends and members of my own family. Although I wish I could believe in their annihilation or conditional immortality or that God would save them in spite of themselves, the Scriptures do not allow such a position. So I pray, trusting in the goodness and wisdom of God, who knows the hearts of all men and women and whose discernment far outweighs my own. Who am I to question what He has set in place? I am the messenger, not the message or its drafter.

## Conclusion

Throughout history, pluralism in its many facets has been helpful in a context of peaceful coexistence among differing religions and philosophies. However, the relativistic way in which our postmodern world chooses to deal with pluralism creates problems for those who continue to declare that there is absolute truth and that humanity is responsible to live according to it. This is our moment in history, and God has chosen that we, who are His image-bearers, represent Him honestly and compassionately. We are not called to victory but to faithfulness. Our guide is an inerrant and Holy Scripture, our strength is in the Holy Spirit, and our hope lies beyond these corruptible bodies in the redemptive work of the one and only Savior.

# 7

# SPIRITUAL APOSTASY AND DOCTRINAL CONFUSION IN THE NEW CENTURY

## Mal Couch

Despite the best intentions and desires of those who trust Jesus as Savior, there will come a day of great religious departure—a defection that will leave Christianity with little substance, existing only as a shell without spiritual power and meaning. The New Testament speaks often of this coming day as the apostasy. In the writings of the apostle Paul, especially, it is indicated that the great departure will probably become fully ripe sometime just before the Rapture of the church.

Paul also wrote that this apostasy, in some ways, was already evident in his generation. Although there would be a final climatic apostasy in the last days, there would always be "departures" throughout the church age.

Has there indeed been ongoing apostasy for the last two thousand years? Does it come upon various generations in different ways? Is there apostasy in Christendom today? And how will apostasy be different in the twenty-first century?

Could the next one hundred years be the countdown to this apostasy and the blessed hope, the Rapture of the church? At some point in the next one hundred years, could the prophesied seven-year tribulation fall upon the world?

# Defining Apostasy

## New Testament Use

In its theological meaning with reference to the church, *apostasia* is used only in 2 Thessalonians 2:3. Here Paul writes, "Let no one in any way deceive you, for [the day of the Lord] will not come unless the apostasy comes first." The word *apostasia* is used by Jewish believers in Jerusalem against Paul. They accused him of "teaching all the Jews who are among the Gentiles, to forsake [*hoti apostasian* (the law of)] Moses" (Acts 21:21). We get an additional sense of the word from the related noun form *apostasion*, which is translated three times in the Gospels as "divorcement" (Matt. 5:31, 19:7; Mark 10:4).

One Greek lexicon defines *apostasia* as "rebellion, [or] abandonment."[1] Additionally, the word carries such meanings as "to depart, to stand aloof, to detach, to forsake."[2] Etymologically, in Greek the word is a compound joining the preposition *apo* (away from) and the noun *stasis* (stand). It literally means "to leave or depart from."[3]

In 2 Thessalonians 2:1–12, Paul describes the work of Satan and the Antichrist at the midpoint of the seven-year tribulation. "In accord with the activity of Satan, with all power and signs and false wonders" (v. 9), the "man of lawlessness" will reveal his true colors and take "his seat in the temple of God, displaying himself as being God" (vv. 3b–4).

But the apostle Paul warns the believers in Thessalonica not to be disturbed because the Day of the Lord, the Tribulation, has not come yet (v. 2). Before that day, the "departure" *(apostasia)* must take place first (v. 3a). Paul was saying to the Thessalonian church that they would see an apostasy long before the Antichrist's during the Tribulation. Paul warns that blindness will overtake the professing church, but that blindness to spiritual matters and what is true will have already darkened the moral and biblical senses of those who have rejected Christ.

Since the apostle has already addressed in detail the issue of the Rapture that will come before the great period of wrath, he does not here, writing to that same church, refer again to the fact that the believers will not see the Antichrist.

On the doctrine of apostasy, Charles Ryrie writes that it is "a departure from truth previously accepted, involving the breaking of a professed relationship with God. Apostasy always involves willful leaving of previously known truth and embracing error."[4]

In the final hours of the dispensation of the church, there will be those who have "confessed" biblical truth and who have "professed" a relationship with God. But they will simply be acting out, living a lie, and walking as religious charlatans. Apostasy will be intense in the final days before the Rapture of the church.

## Apostasy Illustrated in Scripture

The apostles John, Peter, and Paul all speak of apostasy, both "now" and "coming," in both later times and in "the last days." Ryrie describes these facts well:

> Beyond any question, apostasy is both present and future in the church. It was present when Paul wrote to Timothy, and Paul looked forward to a future great apostasy distinctive enough to be of the present-future antichrist. There were antichrists present in the church in John's day, and still he looked forward to the coming great Antichrist (1 John 2:18). Apostasy is something that plagues the church in every generation, though at the end of the church age the great apostasy will come on the scene before the Day of the Lord.[5]

In 1 Timothy 4:1–3, Paul writes that the Spirit "explicitly" speaks of a later-times falling away from the faith. *Falling away* comes from the verb *aphistemi* and can be translated, "they shall dismiss themselves" from the faith. By using the expression "the faith," I believe that the apostle is saying they will remove themselves from the faith profession. These people are not really believers in Christ. Paul continues that they will be "paying attention to deceitful spirits and doctrines of demons" after they have "seared in their own conscience as with a branding iron" (vv. 1b–2). Thus, Paul not only writes of later times, but he also seems to write that some of these things were happening at that time to the church. He urges those who "believe and know the truth" (v. 3) and who are good servants of Christ Jesus to be "constantly nourished on the words of faith and [on] sound doctrine which you have been following" (v. 6).

In 2 Timothy 3:1–9, Paul speaks of "the last days" in which difficult times will come (v. 1). He writes that people will be lovers of self and money. He labels the people of that future day revilers, boastful, arrogant, disobedient to parents, ungrateful, unholy, and "lovers of pleasure rather than lovers of God" (vv. 2–4). He adds that they are "holding to a form of godliness, although they have denied its power" (v. 5).

In this passage, too, Paul speaks of a last-days apostasy but also describes a spiritual falling away during the period of his own ministry. In 2 Timothy 4:3–4, the apostle writes: "For the time will come when they will not endure sound doctrine; but wanting to have their ears tickled, they will accumulate for themselves teachers in accordance to their own desires; and will turn away their ears from the truth, and will turn aside to myths."

In 2 Peter 2:1–3, the apostle Peter also writes of false teachers among the faithful who will "secretly introduce destructive heresies, even denying the Master who bought them, bringing swift destruction upon themselves." He speaks of their sensuality, of how they maligned the truth, and of how they exploit with false words (vv. 2–3). He continues this warning in 2 Peter 3:3: "Know this first of all, that in the last days mockers will come with their mocking, following after their own lusts, and saying, 'Where is the promise of His coming? For all continues just as it was from the beginning of creation'" Peter then reminds his readers that the day of judgment and destruction of the ungodly, who have attempted through the ages to mislead the saints, is a certainty (3:7).

John the apostle witnessed other apostasies. He writes about an early form of Gnosticism, the new cult that believed in secret knowledge and held that Jesus surely could not have had a physical human body, because flesh is sinful. John warns the churches to test the spirits (1 John 4:1). He reminds believers that those who confess that Christ came in the flesh are from God (4:2), "and every spirit that does not confess Jesus is not from God" (v. 3a).

John adds that the spirit of Antichrist is coming, is, in fact, "already in the world" (v. 3b). His summary warning is "Whoever denies the Son does not have the Father; the one who confesses the Son has the Father also" (2:23).

John writes that there will be much apostasy, and it will choke the life from the churches. He speaks of the Nicolaitans (Rev. 2:15), and the cultic immorality of a Jezebel that destroys the strength of churches, such as the one at Thyatira (vv. 20–23). Yet God will preserve the truth and work out His eternal purposes. The church will survive, though awash and nearly drowned in a sea of false teachings.

## *Through the Church Age*

The church suffered persecution almost continually until the emperor Constantine issued the Edict of Milan in January 313. He wrote that "the Christians among the rest, have the liberty to observe the religion of his choice, and his peculiar mode of worship."

Before this freedom, the cults abounded and thrived. One would imagine that in a new climate of safety Christendom would flourish in spiritual purity. It did not. In this reborn atmosphere of tolerance, apostate cults continued and others sprang up. Examples include:

- Ebionites were judaizing disciples who brought many back under the Law of Moses. They rejected what Paul taught, viewed Christ as a mere man, and used only Matthew in a mutilated form.
- The Gnostic-like cult of Cerinthus who made a distinction between the earthly Jesus and the heavenly Christ. His views spread throughout Asia Minor.
- The Pseudo-Clementine Homilies proclaimed that God dwelt on high in bodily form, and His spiritual image could be seen in humans here below. The writings also speak of a feminine side to God.

Although at first glance this ledger of events seems bleak, the true church marched on. There were always thousands who refused to believe the lie. Their faith was protected by the Holy Spirit, who gave them grace and stability to withstand the onslaught of doctrinal confusion.

But a systematized apostasy soon developed and took deep roots as the bishop of Rome came to exert more control than other sectors of the church. The medieval church, which finally came to be called the Roman Catholic Church, was born. With small steps leading to giant steps, a system began to develop that would become forged in iron. A hierarchy of bishops would take control of the church. This organization would be notably powerful in the Roman bishop. A similar set of heresies took root in the churches of the Eastern Roman Empire, who came to compete with—and in the eleventh century split from—Western Christianity.

Doctrinal deviations would grow to include baptismal regeneration, Mariolatry (Mary proclaimed the mother of God, Mary as the co-mediator with Christ), the Mass as a sacrifice of Christ, purgatory, sainthood, prayers for the dead, papal infallibility, forgiveness of sins by the priest, works salvation, and many other antibiblical heresies.

Although it would take centuries for all of this apostate teaching to mature and take center stage, by the time Martin Luther (1483–1546) posted his Ninety-five Theses in 1517, Roman Catholicism was the epitome of departure from the truth.

Many courageous men and women understood from Scripture that the Roman Church was apostate and even pagan in its doctrines. They stood up against the system, and thousands paid with their lives. A few of the more notable martyrs who heeded the Word of God over the teachings of men were Jan Hus (1373–1415), Girolamo Savonarola (1452–1498), and William Tyndale (c. 1494–1536).

Catholicism remained almost intact, with a few minor reforms along the way, while the light of the Reformation blazed brightly. Slowly that Reformation torch of truth was extinguished. Meanwhile, Vatican II Catholicism put on a new face in the latter part of the twentieth century and beckoned its wayward Protestant sheep home. And many fell victim to her seduction.

## The Apostasy of Humanism

While one kind of apostasy flourished in the medieval church, the Renaissance revived another apostasy out of ancient Greek culture. From roots established in the early universities and complex social, political, philosophical, and technological upheavals during the 1400s, Europe found a new, dynamic spirit in the secular Italian Renaissance movement. Humanist artists put the human at the center of life and art, producing glorious sculptures, paintings, and buildings. Florence was the center of this creativity.

Even though a favorite subject for art continued to be religious symbolism, the purpose of the new humanities was to glorify humankind. In the tradition of Plato, the Renaissance artisans sought the ideal in humans and in all that humans could create. Neoplatonism (new Platonism) taught that the soul could ascend toward union with God by contemplating beauty. As a result, a spiritual mysticism swept Europe.

Some thinkers resisted the trends, yet even some of them only hammered out their own system of humanism. For example, Cardinal Nicholas of Cusa's (1401–1464) philosophy stressed the limits of human beings in trying to come to a knowledge of God. He believed that we discover God only through our intuition—through our insights and reasoning processes.

Writing on the dignity of human beings, the philosopher Giovanni Pico della Mirandola (1463–1494) stressed that people can be reborn to a higher life and become more like God. To the human being is granted "to have whatever it chooses, to be whatever it wills."[6]

Technology and industry combined with humanism in the eighteenth and nineteenth centuries to give rise to the Enlightenment and from there theological liberalism. Thus, if humankind can overcome poverty and disease by its own creativity, there is no need for God, so at first, the Scriptures were attacked, then doctrinal Christianity. It was argued that the genius of humanity made the Bible, traditional morality, and God obsolete. At the turn of the twentieth century, such thinking began to gain a serious hearing in many religious circles.

## The "New" Humanism

At the beginning of the twentieth century in Europe, the Reformation of Calvin and Luther was but a shadow of its former self. A very traditional Catholicism held sway on the continent of Europe, especially in southern Europe. Protestantism was basically political and existed generally in lifeless state churches.

Liberalism dominated biblical studies. Theology was taught almost exclusively on the campuses of the state-controlled universities where skepticism had long polluted the spiritual climate. The Bible was torn apart by intellectual criticism. The reasoning of humans had replaced the reasoning of God.

Liberalism and humanism had simultaneously crept across the ocean to North America. Already in the 1700s the young colleges along the Eastern Seaboard of the United States were imbibing Unitarianism, universalism, and other faddish forms of skepticism. By the twentieth century they had become the most prestigious "Ivy League" schools and were long since lost to meaningful faith. By the 1860s, the decade of the American Civil War, whole denominations were slipping away from their biblical roots. The liberals would argue that there was good reason to be optimistic when one looked at the achievements of the human race. Godly faith became a matter of serving and reforming society.

With what was taking place, Unitarians, liberals, and true Christians realized that Christianity was approaching an era of great and irreversible change. The skeptics were calling it a "religious revolution." Edward Ames of the University of Chicago likened it to the bloody peasant revolts that turned Europe on its head in the fourteenth and again in the sixteenth centuries.[7] Others were asking those who were religious to believe in themselves, in the dignity of men, or in the greatness of the human soul.

Still others were arguing that we must ascribe divinity to humans, since it is believed that human nature is one with God's nature, and we need simply awake to that supposed fact. To many, these thoughts were not shocking because the authority of Scripture had already been undercut by the work of so-called objective science. "We are gradually drifting away from the idea that the Bible has any special significance or authority," said John Horsch.[8]

The British evangelist and preacher Charles Haddon Spurgeon (1834–1892) saw where all of this was going when he wrote, "If we have in the Word of God no infallible standard of truth, we are at sea without a compass, and no danger from rough weather without can be equal to this loss within."[9]

In 1915, conservative Bible scholar J. Gresham Machen foresaw the victory of liberalism. "Let us not deceive ourselves," he wrote. "The Bible is at the foundation of the church. Undermine that foundation, and the church will fall."[10] In the 1920s, Arthur Pink also saw changes coming. The trend, he wrote, was the deification of the creature rather than the glorification of God. Rationalism had permeated Christendom. Darwinism and naturalistic evolutionary assumptions about life had taken over the culture and much of the church.

Pink noted as well how widespread the effects of unscriptural teaching in the churches was. He wrote that the craving of his day was for something light and spicy from the pulpit. There was little demand upon the hearts and mental powers of believers.

Apostasy was changing how American and British Christians were thinking, Pink added. He thought that the spiritual climate was such that study of the deeper things of God was about over in church settings. False teachers with their injurious beliefs would follow shortly behind.[11] And he was right. By mid-century, most of the Protestant denominations had capitulated to liberalism and had apostatized to some degree or another.

### The Final Apostasy?

During this past century, behaviorism, pantheism, and evolution have ripped at the very foundation of biblical Christianity. The last fifty years of the twentieth century have been traumatic for the church of Jesus Christ. Could it be that this is actually the first stage for the beginning of the apostasy, that final great deception just prior to the Rapture of the church? Though no one can be dogmatic, forces now in place could signal this possibility.

All of these seeds were planted in the 1700s and 1800s. With Sigmund Freud (1856–1939) and his psychological worldview came an avalanche of behavioral theories that operated from the presumption that human personality and mental process were mechanistic results of physical causes. Human volition and responsibility are denied. With the most blatant of the new psychological systems, behaviorism, the human soul was totally denied and humanity was seen as just one more species of animal. God was "bowed out of existence."[12]

Even evangelical seminaries were adapting secular psychology for their pastoral counseling courses by the 1980s. This "integration" combined secular theories with biblical principles. Many evangelical seminaries that were at one time doctrinally solid, now give advanced degrees in counseling with these secular theories. Counseling centers that are extremely humanistic and eclectic in practice have been established in churches. The average Christian seeking help feels safe in this cocoon of "professionalism." The rhetoric of self-esteem, self-actualization, and self-love is easy to accept. Behaviorism also appeals to the secular mentality. It gets rid of God. It makes human beings less morally responsible, consequences are minimized, and there is no authority to answer to that is higher than self. Behaviorism in the twentieth century has been packaged differently by a variety of successors to Freud, among them Carl Jung, Alfred Adler, Karen Horney, and Erik Erikson. Perhaps the most important name for this list is Carl Rogers.

Born in Oak Park, Illinois in 1902, Rogers had spiritual leanings, but this seems to have been shattered at the age of twenty. Deciding that Jesus was just another man, he gave up plans to be a missionary, and in 1931 received his Ph.D. in psychology. Rogers pioneered the concepts that became known as "self-actualization." Experience, he decided, was the highest authority, higher than the Bible, and higher than Freud or anyone's research. Neither the revelations of God nor man, he said, could take precedence over his own subjective experience.

Rogers believed that humans should trust their feelings over their senses or intellect. The only reality one can possibly know, he concluded, is what the senses experience at the given moment. No experience could be labeled "sinful" or "naughty" and thus clash with one's full awareness. Self-worth should be considered greater than the cultural mores or attitudes. What is right for me is right.

Rogerian philosophy and psychology altered the landscape of society through dominance of the ideas in universities. Here was the foundation for the "Me Generation" of the late century. Does this not remind us of Paul's words that humans are "lovers of self, lovers of money, boastful, arrogant, revilers, disobedient to parents, ungrateful, unholy, unloving, irreconcilable, malicious gossips, without self-control, brutal, haters of good, treacherous, reckless, conceited, lovers of pleasure rather than lovers of God" (2 Tim. 3:1–4)?

## 1990s Spiritual Revival?

In the mid-1990s, a CBS television drama series called "Touched by an Angel" became a hit. Millions of people glued themselves to their TV sets as very human angels who rarely referred to God (at least the God of Scripture) helped humans out of precarious situations. Rabbi Mark Bleiweiss quickly saw the self-indulgence of the program and caught the stupidity of it all in a brilliantly written satire entitled "Slugged by an Angel." He wrote that these "angels are mainly of the savior variety, rescuing their charges from hijackings and hurricanes as well as from the perils of long lines and varicose veins. They're God's little seraphs for the self-indulgent."[13]

Bleiweiss noted that one CBS television executive justified this sorry pot of cold gruel by arguing that there was a growing trend in spirituality and even a mainstream religious revival in the 1990s. Apparently thinking of such forces as Rogers, Bleiweiss concluded:

> Modern angels, far from reuniting us with our Maker, sugar-coat the profound religious alienation in the world today. Angels of prime time iconography are little more than fairy godmothers with an affirmation action attitude. . . . No doubt many folks are bothered by the consuming emptiness of their lives, but not enough to do much about it. [Such angels] are the antithesis of the modern media heroes who make us feel so good about ourselves that serious spiritual reckoning seems somehow beneath us. God is eternity's "Good Guy."[14]

As the twenty-first century begins, we find that the New Age movement is wrapped in all kinds of techniques for the self to find its way to God. New Age philosophy does not promote sacrifice of self but the fulfillment of self. An altered state of consciousness through meditation can put one into harmony with himself or herself and the universe but not with the God of Scripture. Transcendental meditation is more fashionable than ever. The Unification Church promises thousands a spiritual redemption that even Jesus was not able to complete.

Pampering this Eastern movement promises a new world through psychics, astrologers, goddess worship, holistic health, and ecology. Its followers are told to be happy and fulfilled by whatever technique is most helpful for actualization.

Marianne Williamson's book, *A Course in Miracles*, has sold 1 million copies since 1976. The book boasts that "no religion has a monopoly on the greatest story ever told," and that "truth is in all religions." Williamson writes that our ultimate reality is the core of who we are (shades of Carl Rogers).

Thus the apostasy continues, with millions being sucked into the vortex of a new religion of selfism. The people are taught that Christ is but the common thread of divine love in every human mind. Within our minds there is no place where God stops and we begin. Love is but an energy, an infinite continuum.

## Could the Rapture of the Church Be Next?

The Rapture of the church is not simply a doctrine of easy escapism. Instead, the church—those who belong to Christ and are part of the body of Christ—is removed from this earth prior to the impending wrath of God that will be poured out upon a rebellious and self-driven humanity.

The wrath will fall upon last-day mockers who follow after their own lusts and deny the promise of the return of Christ (2 Peter 3:3–4).

It seems clear that the Bible teaches the pretribulation Rapture of the church. That is, all believers who are alive when the Rapture takes place will be lifted up from the earth. The dead in Christ will go first (1 Thess. 4:16), and "then we who are alive and remain shall be caught up together with them in the clouds to meet the Lord in the air, and thus we shall always be with the Lord" (v. 17).

Paul speaks of the Day of the Lord as the wrath (1 Thess. 5:2) and clearly promises that, for all believers alive at that time, "God has not destined us for wrath, but for obtaining salvation [deliverance] through our Lord Jesus Christ" (v. 9). The wrath is the seven-year period of tribulation so vividly described in the book of Revelation. From the beginning, those events that are up front in the Tribulation are collectively called "the wrath." This wrath originates from God who sits on His throne and from the Savior, Christ the Lamb (Rev. 6:16–17).

With great zeal and anticipation, the apostle Paul further describes the Rapture of the church with these words: "Behold, I tell you a mystery; we shall not all sleep, but we shall be all changed, in a moment, in the twinkling of an eye, at the last trumpet; for the trumpet will sound, and the dead will be raised imperishable, and we shall be changed. For this perishable must put on imperishable, and this mortal must put on immortality" (1 Cor. 15:51–53).

## The Promised Wrath of God

How terrible it will be for family members, friends, and neighbors to have missed the Rapture of the church. They will be forced to enter a horrible period known as "the great world tribulation" and feel the wrath of God.

The answer to the question "What will bring on the Rapture of the church and then the wrath?" seems to be found in what is happening in the hearts of people on earth. They will have turned to selfism and humanism like no other generation before.

Paul writes of a stubborn and unrepentant heart that stores up for itself in the day of judgment (Rom. 2:5). He speaks of selfish ambition and tribulation and distress "for every soul of man who does evil" (vv. 8–9). And finally he writes, because of all kinds of sins, "passion, evil desire, and greed, . . . the wrath of God will come" (Col. 3:5–6).

## What Should We Be Doing?

Paul writes to the persecuted church at Thessalonica, lauding them for their rejection of idolatry and their expectancy for Christ's return (1 Thess. 1:9–10). They were active and looking for the return of Jesus. They were serving and waiting. This is the message for Christians at the beginning of the twenty-first century.

Since we can never be sure when God's purposes for His church will be finalized, we must remain obedient to our Lord's commands. This was made clear to the disciples at the time of Christ's ascension to heaven. They had asked if He was going to restore the kingdom to Israel at that time, and Jesus told them, "It is not for you to know the times or epochs which the Father has fixed by His own authority" (Acts 1:7). Two facts are clear in this statement: First, the date has been set, and second, we aren't supposed to know it because we have a responsibility to fulfill in the meantime.[15]

Though he would probably not believe all of our scenario about the return of the Lord, the godly Scottish pastor Samuel Rutherford (1600–1661) still held a great living hope of seeing the Lord bring all things to a blessed conclusion. In 1648, he wrote to a dying friend, George Gillespie:

> The night, you say, is dark and long,
> The city out of sight;
> Yet lift your eyes: look to the east
> Where shadows take their flight.
> And though the goal seem wreathed in mists
> Still cleave to Christ your Guide
> Whose hidden love reserves for you
> Those comforts now denied.
> But one fight more—one fight of faith—

The bravest and the last;
One act of firm believing then
The conflict shall be past.
On Christ's strong righteousness rely
Nor gaze on all your sin;
Grace signs each debt as fully paid,
Declares the guilty clean.
To Him commit your deathless soul,
Your weakness to His strength,
Until your faltering steps shall gain
Immanuel's land at length.[16]

# ENDNOTES

## Chapter 1

1. James Orr, *The Christian View of God and the World* (Edinburgh: Andrew Elliot, 1897), 4.
2. David A. Noebel, *Understanding the Times: The Religious Worldviews of Our Day and the Search for Truth* (Eugene, Ore.: Harvest House, 1991).
3. R. J. Rummel, *Death by Government* (New Brunswick, N.J.: Transaction Publishers, 1994), 9.
4. Ibid., 13.
5. Gene Edward Veith Jr., *Modern Fascism: Liquidating the Judeo-Christian Worldview* (St. Louis: Concordia, 1993), 137.
6. Arthur Herman, *The Idea of Decline in Western History* (New York: Free Press, 1997), 349.
7. Ibid., 357.
8. Ibid., 79.
9. Lawrence E. Cahoone, ed., *From Modernism to Postmodernism: An Anthology* (Cambridge: Blackwell, 1996), 20.
10. David Horowitz, *The Weekly Standard*, 9 March 1998, 35.
11. David Horowitz, *Radical Son: A Journey Through Our Times* (New York: Free Press, 1997), 405. For those interested in further study in this particular area, see Martin Jay, *The Dialectical Imagination: A History of the Frankfurt School and the Institute of Social Research, 1923–1950* (Berkeley and Los Angeles: University of California Press, 1973) for the background on critical theory. Marxist Theodor W. Adorno's *The Authoritarian Personality* is continually used to paint conservatives as fascists and Nazis. For a discussion of this book see Ludwig von Mises, *Socialism* (Indianapolis: Liberty Classics, 1981), 523.

12. James C. Dobson and Gary L. Bauer, *Children at Risk* (Dallas: Word, 1990), 22.

13. Ibid., 182. See John A. Stormer, *None Dare Call It Education* (Florissant, Mo.: Liberty Bell, 1998), on why capitalism is ridiculed, family values attacked, and American history rewritten.

14. Richard John Neuhaus, *The Naked Public Square: Religion and Democracy in America* (Grand Rapids: Eerdmans, 1986). Nancy R. Pearcey and Charles B. Thaxton, *The Soul of Science: Christian Faith and Natural Philosophy* (Wheaton, Ill.: Crossway, 1994), 19: "In the late nineteenth century [c. 1893] England, several small groups of scientists and scholars organized under the leadership of Thomas H. Huxley to overthrow the cultural dominance of Christianity—particularly the intellectual dominance of the Anglican church. Their goal was to secularize society, replacing the Christian worldview with scientific naturalism, a worldview that recognizes the existence of nature alone." The British Fabian Society was also heavily involved in replacing Christianity with socialism. According to M. Margaret McCarran, "Socialism was demonstrably conceived as a universal 'religion' and 'faith' . . . based on the religion of scientific humanism." M. Margaret McCarran, *Fabianism in the Political Life of Britain, 1919–1931* (Chicago: Heritage Foundation, 1954), 50.

15. David C. Large, *Where Ghosts Walked: Munich's Road to the Third Reich* (New York: W. W. Norton, 1997), 245.

16. Erwin W. Lutzer, *Hitler's Cross* (Chicago: Moody, 1995), 61.

17. See Arthur Herman, *The Idea of Decline in Western History* (New York: Free Press, 1997), 46–75, for an excellent summary of Gobineau's ideas on race.

18. "'Whoever wants to understand National Socialist Germany must know Wagner,' Hitler used to say." *Hitler's Cross*, 80.

19. *Modern Fascism*, 140.

20. *Where Ghosts Walked*, 245–46.

21. Ibid., 76–77.

22. *Socialism*, 530.

23. Stanley G. Payne, *A History of Fascism, 1914–1945* (Madison, Wis.: University of Wisconsin Press, 1995), 484.

24. A. E. Wilder-Smith, *Man's Origin, Man's Destiny* (Minneapolis: Bethany Fellowship, 1968), 187.

25. Ibid., 190.

26. Phillip E. Johnson, *Reason in the Balance: The Case against Naturalism in Science, Law and Education* (Downers Grove, Ill.: InterVarsity, 1995).

27. *Man's Origin, Man's Destiny*, 190–91.

28. Ian T. Taylor, *In the Minds of Men: Darwin and the New World Order* (Toronto: TFE, 1984), 409.

29. For a complete understanding of socialism, we recommend Ludwig von Mises' work, *Socialism*.

30. Friedrich A. Hayek, *The Road to Serfdom* (Chicago: University of Chicago Press, 1944), 28.

31. Richard Vetterli and William E. Fort, Jr., *The Socialist Revolution* (Los Angeles: Clute International Corp., 1968), 88.

32. Hans Kohn, *The Mind of Germany* (New York: Scribner, 1960).

33. Vetterli and Fort, *The Socialist Revolution*, 87; *Modern Fascism*, 59–60.

34. Ibid.

35. John Robbins, *The Trinity Review*, February 1998.

36. Ibid.

37. Ibid.

38. Delitzsch, a biblical scholar at the University of Berlin, "published a book arguing that the Old Testament was dependent upon Babylonian culture and mythology." In a later work, he concluded that "the Old Testament was full of deceptions of all kinds—a veritable hodgepodge of erroneous, incredible, undependable figures, including those of Biblical chronology." See Veith, *Modern Fascism*, 53–54.

39. *Modern Fascism*, 61–62. Veith gives an excellent summary of the role of the theologians in the rise of Hitler's National Socialism.

40. *The Dialectical Imagination*, 24–25. For an insightful look at Tillich, we recommend Hannah Tillich's *From Time to Time* (New York: Spein and Day, 1973). Tillich was not only a radical Marxist theologian but also a libertine. Surprisingly,

Tillich is also considered a key theologian to at least one conservative religious denomination. See H. Ray Dunning's *Grace, Faith and Holiness* (Kansas City, Mo.: Beacon Hill, 1988).

41. *Hitler's Cross*, 196.

42. Franklin H. Littell and Hubert G. Locke, eds., *The German Church Struggle and the Holocaust* (Detroit: Wayne State University Press, 1974), 24; quoted in *Modern Fascism*, 71.

43. Michael J. Wilkins and J. P. Moreland, *Jesus Under Fire: Modern Scholarship Reinvents the Historical Jesus* (Grand Rapids: Zondervan, 1995), 145.

44. *A History of Fascism, 1914–1945*, 485–86.

45. *Man's Origin, Man's Destiny*, 191.

46. Ibid., 186.

47. *Modern Fascism*, 17.

48. *Socialism*, 530. "Hitler . . . failed even in the lower grades of high school. He never had any honest job. It is a fable that he had ever been a paperhanger. . . . He was a maniac obsessed by megalomania."

49. Ibid., 20.

50. Z. Dobbs, *The Great Deceit: Social Pseudo-Sciences* (West Sayville, N.Y.: Veritas Foundation, 1964), 143.

51. Ibid., 144.

52. The American counterpart to the British Fabian Society was the League for Industrial Democracy and was headed for years by socialist John Dewey, father of secular humanist education in the United States. Among the League's participants was Morris Hillquit, head of the Socialist Party in the 1920s and "a militant defender of the Bolshevik Revolution and a vociferous supporter of the Communist International." Dobbs, *The Great Deceit*, 26. Sponsors of the L.I.D. included Senators Jacob Javits, Paul H. Douglas, Wayne Morse, and others.

53. Bernard Shaw, *Intelligent Woman's Guide to Socialism* (New York: Brentanno, 1928), 470. Cited in *The Great Deceit*, 144.

54. *Modern Fascism*, 26: "Part of the problem in recognizing fascism is the assumption that it is conservative. Sternhell has observed how study of the ideology has been obscured by 'the official Marxist interpretation of fascism.' . . . The

influence of Marxist scholarship has severely distorted our understanding of fascism. Communism and fascism were rival brands of socialism." *Socialism,* 523: "It is of much greater consequence that the Communists have succeeded in changing the semantic connotation of the term *Fascism.* Fascism, as will be shown later, was a variety of Italian socialism. If one wants to assign Fascism and Nazism to the same class of political systems, one must call this class a dictatorial regime and one must not neglect to assign the Soviets to the same class. In recent years the Communists' semantic innovations have gone even further. They call everybody whom they dislike, every advocate of the free enterprise system, a Fascist."

55. *The Socialist Revolution,* 57.
56. *Socialism,* 525.
57. Ibid. See also *The Socialist Revolution,* 58.
58. *The Socialist Revolution,* 68.
59. Gene Edward Veith, Jr., *Postmodern Times: A Christian Guide to Contemporary Thought and Culture* (Wheaton, Ill.: Crossway, 1994). Dennis McCallum, ed., *The Death of Truth* (Minneapolis: Bethany House, 1996). Thomas C. Oden, *After Modernity . . . What?* (Grand Rapids: Zondervan, 1990).
60. The Marxist-Leninist worldview is covered in greater detail in *Understanding the Times.*
61. For example, Rummel in *Death by Government,* 46, tells of Khorassan in Persia, "scene of a carnival of blood scarcely surpassed even in Mongol annals. . . . Separate piles of heads of men, women, and children were built into pyramids; and even cats and dogs were killed in the streets. An utterly fantastic 1,747,000 human beings reportedly were slaughtered."
62. Ibid., 8.
63. Joseph Stalin, *Works* (Moscow and London: n.p., 1952–1953) 1:304.
64. Karl Marx, *The Communist Manifesto* (Chicago: Henry Regnery, 1954), 30.
65. Ibid., 53.
66. Ibid., 54.
67. Jacques Barzun, *Darwin, Marx, Wagner* (Garden City, N.Y.: Doubleday, 1958), 8.

68. Georg W. F. Hegel, *Philosophy of History* (1832), cited in John Bartlett, *Familiar Quotations* (Boston: Little, Brown, 1955), 401.

69. V. I. Lenin, *Collected Works* (Moscow: Progress, 1978), 10:86.

70. Ibid., 35:122.

71. Hans Küng, *Does God Exist?* (Garden City, N.Y.: Doubleday, 1980), 257.

72. Quoted in Whittaker Chambers, *Witness* (New York: Random House, 1952), 712.

73. For a full account of dialectical materialism see *Understanding the Times*, chap. 7.

74. Karl Marx and Frederick Engles, *Selected Correspondence* (New York: International Publishers, 1924), 125.

75. Frederick Engles, *Selected Works* (1950), 2:153. Cited in R. N. Carew Hunt, *The Theory and Practice of Communism* (Baltimore: Penguin, 1966), 64.

76. V. I. Lenin, *Materialism and Empirio-Criticism* (New York: International Publishers, 1927), 34.

77. *Communist Manifesto*, 27.

78. Ibid., 54.

79. Ibid., 33.

80. V. I. Lenin, *Selected Works* (New York: International Publishers, 1937), 9:479.

81. Karl Marx and Frederick Engels, *Collected Works*, 40 vols. (New York: International Publishers, 1976), 6:494–95.

82. Lenin, *Selected Works*, 10:91, 92.

83. Karl Marx, *Civil War in France* (New York: International Publishers, 1937), 19.

84. Malachi Martin, *The Keys of This Blood* (New York: Simon and Schuster, 1990), 177.

85. Nikita Khrushchev, "Ukrainian Bulletin," 1–15 August, 1960, 12. Cited in James Bales, *Communism and the Reality of Moral Law* (Nutley, N.J.: Craig, 1969), 121.

86. *From Modernism to Postmodernism*, 10.

87. John Dewey, *A Common Faith* (New Haven: Yale University Press, 1934), 87. For forty-five exhibits proving that secular humanism is a religion see David A. Noebel, *Clergy in the Classroom* (Manitou Springs, Colo.: Summit, 1995). One of the exhibits is from the Harvard University Gazette

newspaper (9 July 1993), which admits that secular humanism is a religion and its humanist chaplain at Harvard is Thomas Ferrick.

88. Elasah Drogin, *Margaret Sanger: Father of Modern Society* (New Hope, Ky.: CUL, 1986), 9.
89. Ibid., 38.
90. Ibid., 87.
91. Lena Levine, "Planned Parenthood News," summer 1953, 10.
92. Sherri Tepper, *You've Changed the Combination* (Denver: Rocky Mountain Planned Parenthood, 1974).
93. George Grant, *Grand Illusions* (Brentwood, Tenn.: Wolgemuth and Hyatt, 1988), 49.
94. *Margaret Sanger*, 10.
95. *Grand Illusions*, 96.
96. *Margaret Sanger*, 94–95. For those interested in Margaret Sanger and her Planned Parenthood organization, which is still funded by the U.S. government, we strongly recommend Grant's book, *Grand Illusions*.
97. Charles Francis Potter, *Humanism: A New Religion* (New York: Simon and Schuster, 1930), 128.
98. "Among religions in this country which do not teach what would generally be considered a belief in the existence of God are Buddhism, Taoism, Ethical Culture, secular humanism and others." U. S. Supreme Court, "Torcaso v. Watkins," 19 June 1961.
99. For additional information on America's educational leftward slant from John Dewey through George Counts, Harold Rugg, Benjamin Bloom, and on to Brock Chisholm and Chester Pierce, see *None Dare Call It Education*.
100. Paul Kurtz, *The Humanist Alternative* (Buffalo, N.Y.: Prometheus, 1973), 177.
101. Corliss Lamont, quoted in Roger E. Greeley, ed., *The Best of Humanism* (Buffalo, N.Y.: Prometheus, 1988), 149.
102. William Provine, "The Scientist," 5 September 1988, 10.
103. Carl Sagan, *The Dragons of Eden* (New York: Random House, 1977), 6.
104. "Carl Rogers," *Journal of Humanistic Psychology*, Summer 1982, 8.
105. Lawrence Casler, "The Humanist," March–April 1974, 4.

106.   Delos B. McKown, "The Humanist," May–June 1989, 24.

107.   Julian Huxley, "The Humanist," March–April 1979, 35.

108.   *The Humanist Manifesto* (Buffalo, N.Y.: Prometheus, 1980), 10.

109.   Will and Ariel Durant, *The Lessons of History* (New York: Simon and Schuster, 1968), 18.

110.   Ibid., 81.

111.   *Hitler's Cross*, 205.

112.   Ibid., 201.

113.   Ibid., 173–74.

114.   For a defense of the Christian worldview, see, for example, *Understanding the Times;* Carl F. H. Henry, *God, Revelation and Authority*, 6 vols. (Dallas: Word, 1976–1983); Ronald H. Nash, *Worldviews in Conflict: Choosing Christianity in a World of Ideas* (Grand Rapids: Zondervan, 1992); W. Gary Phillips and William E. Brown, *Making Sense of Your World* (Chicago: Moody, 1991); J. P. Moreland, *Love Your God with All Your Mind* (Colorado Springs, Colo.: NavPress, 1997); Wilkins and Moreland, *Jesus Under Fire;* Norman L. Geisler, *Christian Apologetics* (Grand Rapids: Baker, 1997); Norman L. Geisler and Thomas Howe, *When Critics Ask* (Grand Rapids: Baker, 1992); Norman L. Geisler and Ron Brooks, *When Skeptics Ask: A Handbook on Christian Evidences* (Grand Rapids: Baker, 1996); Norman L. Geisler, *Christian Ethics: Options and Issues* (Grand Rapids: Baker, 1990); Norman L. Geisler and Frank Turek, *Legislating Morality* (Minneapolis: Bethany House, 1998).

115.   *Hitler's Cross*, 204.

## Chapter 2

1.   D. A. Lyon, "Technology," in *The New Dictionary of Christian Ethics and Pastoral Theology*, ed. David J. Atkinson and David H. Field (Downers Grove, Ill.: InterVarsity Press, 1995), 835.

2.   David C. Lindberg, *The Beginnings of Western Science: The European Scientific Tradition in Philosophical, Religious, and Institutional Context, 600 B.C. to A.D. 1450* (Chicago: University of Chicago Press, 1992), 149–52.

3.   Georges Duby, *The Age of the Cathedrals: Art and Society, 980–1420*, trans. Eleanor Levieux and Barbara Thompson (Chicago: University of Chicago Press, 1981), 146–65.

4.  For much of the framework and thought of this chapter, I am indebted to Stephen V. Monsma et al., *Responsible Technology: A Christian Perspective* (Grand Rapids: Eerdmans, 1986).

5.  For a critique from a perspective that sees technology as having a negative economic impact globally, see Jeremy Rifkin, *The End of Work* (New York: Putnam's, 1995). For an evaluation of technology's unintended consequences in society, see Edward Tenner, *Why Things Bite Back* (New York: Vintage Books, 1996).

6.  *The End of Work*, 42.

7.  Ibid., 44. Rifkin further argues that during the last half of the nineteenth century, there was an ideological shift due to technology. As a result, "the technological vision had succeeded in converting the American masses from foot soldiers for the Lord to factors of production and from sentient beings created in the likeness of God to tools fashioned in the image of machines" (44–45).

8.  Notable exceptions to this trend are Monsma, *Responsible Technology*, and Egbert Schuurman, *Technology and the Future: A Philosophical Challenge* (Toronto: Wedge, 1980). From a broader Christian perspective, two excellent works are Carl Mitcham and Jim Grote, eds., *Theology and Technology: Essays in Christian Analysis and Exegesis* (Lanham, Md.: University Press of America, 1984), and David H. Hopper, *Technology, Theology, and the Idea of Progress* (Louisville, Ky.: Westminster/John Knox, 1991).

9.  *Responsible Technology*, 43–44.

10. Carl F. H. Henry, *New Strides of Faith* (Chicago: Moody, 1972), 129, 132.

11. The issue of high-technology warfare and the ethics of warfare, especially the Christian tradition of just war, are beyond the scope of this chapter but should not be overlooked. Technology is once again transforming the battlefield and raising crucial questions that need a biblical response.

12. Ian Barbour, *Ethics in an Age of Technology* (San Francisco: HarperCollins, 1993), 3.

13. Charles Susskind, *Understanding Technology* (Baltimore: Johns Hopkins University Press, 1973), 132.

14. John Zerman and Alice Carnes, eds., *Questioning Technology* (Santa Cruz, Calif.: New Society Publishers, 1991), 217.

15. C. S. Lewis, *The Abolition of Man* (New York: Macmillan, 1965), 69.
16. *Ethics in an Age of Technology*, 4–8.
17. Ibid., 8–10.
18. Ibid., 10–12.
19. Ibid., 12–15.
20. Ibid., 15.
21. Ibid., 15.
22. Ibid., 18.
23. For a presentation on technology and justice, see George P. Grant, *Technology and Justice* (Notre Dame: University of Notre Dame Press, 1986).
24. David W. Gill, "Technology," in Robert Banks and R. Paul Stevens, eds., *The Complete Book of Everyday Christianity* (Downers Grove, Ill.: InterVarsity, 1997), 1017.
25. Ibid., 833.
26. Ibid., 834.
27. *Responsible Technology*, 49.
28. "Technology," 834.
29. *Responsible Technology*, 50, 58.
30. Ibid., 162. On a similar note, Schuurman writes of the Reformation and its biblical perspective, "What one finds in the Reformation is an effort to return to the original command given humanity to dress and keep the creation. The Reformation views nature as *created* nature and has once and for all rejected any deified nature that might be reckoned untouchable. From a Christian standpoint, then, all technology, including modern technology, pertains to the service and glory of God. In modern humanism, however, this view has been secularized so that technology exists for and around humankind. Is it not precisely this that has proven so disruptive, that as autonomous humanity progressively set its stamp upon technological development, technology became an autonomous power set against humanity?" (354).
31. *Responsible Technology*, 200.
32. Ibid., 59–68.
33. Ibid., 62–64.
34. Ibid., 62.
35. Ibid., 65–66.
36. Ibid., 66.

37. Ibid., 68.
38. Ibid., 68–69. Monsma writes: "Thus a starting point is to ask—whether as a researcher, designer, fabricator, distributor, purchaser, or user of a technological object—if that object uses entities from God's creation in a manner that respects their God-given nature and purposes, and if it increases human beings' opportunities to be the joyful, loving, creative beings God intends them to be. Technological activities that are in keeping with the command to love and attempt to meet these two criteria help make possible humanity's search for God's kingdom of shalom, a kingdom of activity, dynamism, and vibrancy, but also a kingdom of peace, harmony, and joy" (69).
39. These seven principles are derived from Monsma's eight principles in *Responsible Technology* (combining information and communication) found on pages 71–76 and 170–77. For another perspective upholding many of the same concerns, see Barbour, *Ethics in an Age of Technology*, 41–46.
40. Robert A. Wauzzinski, "Technological Optimism," *Perspectives on Science and Christian Faith* 48, no. 3 (September 1996): 150.
41. This is not to cast condemnation on the accomplishments or motives of those working in the sciences. Nor is it to deny the sincerity of their efforts or benefits of their work. Scientists Enzo Russo and David Cove write: "The moral obligation of scientists is to inform the general public of the possible ways that scientific knowledge can be used and misused. Decisions over how scientific knowledge is used are independent of the knowledge and should be taken independently. Each of us has the moral obligation to understand more about what scientists are learning, how this scientific knowledge can be transformed into technology, how these new technologies could be misused and what could be done to avoid this potential misuse. This is the price we have to pay for having eaten from the tree of knowledge, as we are reminded in Genesis. To stop scientific research is both impossible and unwise. To slow down technological 'progress' may be very wise." *Genetic Engineering: Dreams and Nightmares* (Oxford: W. H. Freeman, 1995), 207.

42.  Craig M. Gay, *The Way of the (Modern) World* (Grand Rapids: Eerdmans, 1998), 81.

43.  Ibid., 82.

44.  For an overview of some of the issues in bioethics from a Christian perspective, see the BioBasics series, Gary P. Stewart, ed. (Grand Rapids: Kregel, 1998); Timothy J. Demy and Gary P. Stewart, eds., *Genetic Engineering: A Christian Response* (Grand Rapids: Kregel, 1999).

45.  John Polkinghorne, "Cloning and the Moral Imperative," in *Human Cloning: Religious Responses*, ed. Ronald Cole-Turner (Louisville, Ky.: Westminster/John Knox, 1997), 42.

46.  R. Albert Mohler, Jr., "The Brave New World of Cloning: A Christian Worldview Perspective," in *Human Cloning*, 103.

47.  Ibid.

48.  Leo Alexander, "Medical Science under Dictatorship," *New England Journal of Medicine* 241, no. 2 (July 1947): 39–47.

49.  *The End of Work*, 5.

50.  Thomas Ice and Timothy Demy, *The Coming Cashless Society* (Eugene, Ore.: Harvest House, 1996), 152–53.

51.  Alvin Toffler, *Powershift: Knowledge, Wealth, and Violence at the Edge of the Twenty-First Century* (New York: Bantam, 1990), 20.

52.  "The Wired World Atlas," *Wired* (November 1996): 162.

53.  The propensity of some interpreters of prophecy, often within pretribulationism (which is the view this author holds), to seek to identify current technologies and weapons with the vocabulary of the biblical text is misguided and an aberration of consistent hermeneutic principles. At whatever point in human history the final events of Revelation transpire, the technology available at that time will be used. The preoccupation of many prophecy students with technology and the Tribulation has unintentionally undermined premillennialism.

54.  Roger L. Shinn, "Between Eden and Babel," in *Human Cloning*, 117.

55.  "Technology," 1017.

56.  Carl F. H. Henry, *Carl Henry at His Best* (Portland, Ore.: Multnomah, 1989), 28.

57.  Carl Mitchum, "Technology and Ethics: From Expertise to Public Participation," *The World & I* (March 1996): 329.

58.  *Ethics in an Age of Technology*, 223.
59.  *Responsible Technology*, 209–17.
60.  Ibid., 217.
61.  *The Way of the (Modern) World*, 129.
62.  Daniel J. Boorstin, *The Discoverers* (New York: Random House, 1983), 36.

### Chapter 3

1.  Lewis Sperry Chafer, *Systematic Theology*, 8 vols. (Dallas: Dallas Seminary Press, 1948), 2:77.
2.  Robert C. Walton, *Chronological and Background Charts of Church History* (Grand Rapids: Zondervan, 1986), chart 78.
3.  David F. Wells, *No Place for Truth: Or Whatever Happened to Evangelical Theology?* (Grand Rapids: Eerdmans, 1993), 135–36.
4.  Ibid., 7.
5.  Ibid., 95.
6.  Thomas C. Oden, "On Not Whoring After the Spirit of the Age," in *No God But God: Breaking with the Idols of Our Age*, ed. Os Guinness and John Seel (Chicago: Moody, 1992), 8. A book expressing similar concerns is the collection of essays compiled and edited by Michael Horton, *Power Religion: The Selling Out of the Evangelical Church* (Chicago: Moody, 1992).
7.  "On Not Whoring," 193–94.
8.  Ibid.
9.  Rousas John Rushdoony, *Revolt against Maturity* (Fairfax, Va.: Thoburn, 1977), 335.
10.  New York: Macmillan, 1943, 87–88.
11.  Samuel J. Andrews, *Christianity and Anti-Christianity in Their Final Conflict* (Chicago: Bible Institute Colportage Association, 1898), 253–57.
12.  Arthur L. Johnson, *Faith Misguided: Exposing the Dangers of Mysticism* (Chicago: Moody, 1988), 26.
13.  Timothy Crater, "The Filling of the Spirit in the New Testament," (unpub. Th.M. thesis, Dallas Theological Seminary, 1971), 45.
15.  "The Filling," 46.
16.  E. W. Bullinger, *Figures of Speech Used in the Bible* (1898; repr. ed., Grand Rapids: Baker, 1968), 540.

17. See Dwight Allen Ekholm, "The Doctrine of the Christian's Walk in the Spirit," (unpub. Th.M. thesis, Dallas Theological Seminary, 1973).

## Chapter 4

1. David Barton, *America: To Pray or Not to Pray?* (Aledo, Tex.: WallBuilder, 1991), 44.
2. Ibid., 89.
3. Ibid., 9.
4. Alexis de Tocqueville, *Democracy in America*, 2 vols. (New York: Vintage, 1945), 1:23, 314–15, 319.
5. Tim LaHaye, *The Battle for the Mind* (Old Tappan, N.J.: Revell, 1980); and Tim and Beverly LaHaye, *A Nation Without a Conscience* (Wheaton, Ill.: Tyndale, 1994).
6. For more verification of the claims of Christ, see Tim LaHaye, *Jesus, Who Is He?* (Sisters, Ore.: Multnomah, 1997).

## Chapter 5

1. Edward Gordon Selwyn, *The First Epistle of St. Peter*, 2d ed., Thornapple Commentaries (Grand Rapids: Baker, 1981), 174.

## Chapter 6

1. The author, for more than twelve years, has experienced the challenge of this subject. I have labored to provide faithful ministry in an institutional environment, and in so doing, I have remained faithful to my ecclesiastical endorsement, ordination, and evangelical theology. Yet I count as my friends and colleagues many individuals of diverse religious and political backgrounds. These include priests from the Orthodox, Roman Catholic, and Episcopal persuasions; a Jewish rabbi; and numerous Protestant ministers from across the theological spectrum. Also included are many friends and acquaintances from the Armed Forces officer and enlisted communities across an even broader religious spectrum.
2. E. D. Cook, "Pluralism," in David J. Atkinson, David F. Field, Arthur Holmes, and Oliver O'Donovan, eds., *The New Dictionary of Christian Ethics and Pastoral Theology* (Downers Grove, Ill.: InterVarsity, 1995), 666 (emphasis added).

3.  Examples of confusion regarding the actual meaning and application of pluralism abound. The example I have chosen in no way reflects negatively on the author, for his work is excellent. In discussing the moral dilemma that America confronts because of its pluralistic makeup, James Davison Hunter asks, "Are there any limits to pluralism? Is there anything, in other words, that we will not view as acceptable behavior or lifestyle? Should there be any such limits? And on what grounds can a community justify the imposition of limits to pluralism? What compelling reasons, acceptable to all, are there for establishing boundaries between what is acceptable and what is not?" (308). The issue at hand is not pluralism itself but the moral and theological dilemma that pluralism creates. Different philosophies spawn different ethics that come from different morals. The issue here is tolerance: "Are there limits to tolerance?" Should some values or morals be tolerated while others are not? Pluralistic societies need to find practical ways to discern what is good for the society as a whole and what is detrimental. For the full discussion, see James Davison Hunter, *Culture Wars: The Struggle to Define America* (New York: Basic, 1991), 308–12.

4.  D. A. Carson, *The Gagging of God: Christianity Confronts Pluralism* (Grand Rapids: Zondervan, 1996), 13–18. Carson's concept of *cherished pluralism* is simply "an additional ingredient to empirical pluralism." It identifies the good or the gains that come from living in a society that assimilates the views of others into its infrastructure. Again, this term adds to the confusion of the meaning of pluralism— *cherished pluralism* describes more of what people are willing or not willing to tolerate within a pluralistic setting.

5.  S. D. Gaede, *When Tolerance Is No Virtue: Political Correctness, Multiculturalism, and the Future of Truth and Justice* (Downers Grove, Ill.: InterVarsity, 1993), 36.

6.  Gene Edward Veith, Jr., *Postmodern Times: A Christian Guide to Contemporary Thought and Culture* (Wheaton, Ill.: Crossway, 1994), 152. See also, Paul C. Vitz, *Psychology as Religion: The Cult of Self-Worship*, 2d ed. (Grand Rapids: Eerdmans, 1994), 166–68. Vitz argues that "separatist and secessionist movements are surfacing around the globe. Here in America

the question of what can hold us together is on the minds of most thoughtful observers of the social and political scene" (166).

7.  Samuel P. Huntington, "The Erosion of American National Interest," *Foreign Affairs* (September–October 1997): 34–35.

8.  Samuel P. Huntington, *The Clash of Civilizations and the Remaking of World Order* (New York: Simon and Schuster, 1996), 21.

9.  Ibid., 28.

10. Nina Shea, "Atrocities Not Fit to Print," *First Things* (November 1997): 33.

11. Ibid., 33.

12. *The Clash of Civilizations*, 217.

13. *Postmodern Times*, 153.

14. *When Tolerance Is No Virtue*, 17.

15. Ibid., 21. Gaede states that political correctness "allows each group to define tolerance for itself" (21). It seems more accurate to understand tolerance, in a multicultural setting, to be overarching or an umbrella that protects all cultures from raining down perspectives on one another. For tolerance to work, it must be understood similarly by each culture or subculture. If each culture truly defines tolerance itself, it would be contaminated by subjective criteria and therefore, fail to eliminate divisiveness and dissension. Later Gaede appears to correct this statement when he suggests that the only conviction a pluralistic society embraces is "uniform tolerance" (22).

16. Don E. Eberly, *Restoring the Good Society: A New Vision for Politics and Culture* (Grand Rapids: Baker, 1994), 78.

17. *Culture Wars*, 41.

18. *When Tolerance Is No Virtue*, 49.

19. Ibid., 60.

20. Ibid., 74.

21. *Culture Wars*, 325.

22. James F. Childress and John C. Fletcher, "Respect for Autonomy," *Hastings Center Report* (May–June 1994): 35.

23. Margaret Norden, "Whose Life is It Anyway? A study in respect for autonomy," *Journal of Medical Ethics*, 21 (1995): 182.

24. Thomas H. Murray, "Individualism and Community: The Contested Terrain of Autonomy," *Hastings Center Report* (May–June 1994): 33.

25. E. D. Cook, "Autonomy," in *New Dictionary of Christian Ethics and Pastoral Theology*, 180.

26. Gilbert Meilaender, "Our Vocabularies, Our Selves," *Hastings Center Report* (May–June 1994): 14.

27. William D. Watkins, *The New Absolutes: How They Are Being Imposed on Us and How They Are Eroding Our Moral Landscape* (Minneapolis: Bethany House, 1996), 29.

28. This movement sees any form of authority as incompatible with autonomy and possibly represents the purest form of absolute autonomy.

29. H. Wayne House and Kenneth M. Durham, *Living Wisely in a Foolish World: A Contemporary Look at the Wisdom of Proverbs* (Grand Rapids: Kregel Publications, 1992), 186.

30. Willard Gaylin, "Knowing Good and Doing Good," *Hastings Center Report* (May–June 1994): 37.

31. Daniel Callahan, "Bioethics: Private Choice and Common Good," *Hastings Center Report* (May–June 1994): 28.

32. John Hick, "A Pluralist View," in Dennis L. Okholm and Timothy R. Phillips, eds., *Four Views of Salvation in a Pluralistic World* (Grand Rapids: Zondervan, 1995), 38.

33. Ibid., 43.

34. Ibid., 39, 45.

35. W. Gary Phillips, "Evangelical Pluralism: A Singular Problem," *Bibliotheca Sacra* 151 (April–June 1994): 141–42.

36. *The Gagging of God*, 19–26.

37. James D. Chancellor, "Christ and Religious Pluralism," *Review and Expositor* 91 (1994): 542. Chancellor remarks that Muslims and Buddhists have come to an understanding that religious pluralism is inconsistent with their own practices.

38. See John E. Sanders, "Is Belief in Christ Necessary for Salvation?" *Evangelical Quarterly* 60 (1988): 241–59; and Evert D. Osburn, "Those Who Have Never Heard: Have They No Hope?" *Journal of the Evangelical Theological Society* 32 (1989):367–72. Historically, inclusivism is associated with a Roman Catholic theologian, Karl Rahner. He taught that those who respond to whatever light has been given to them will receive the grace of God in salvation. See John B. Cobb Jr., "Being a Transformationist in a Pluralistic World," *The Christian Century*, 10–17 August 1994: 748.

39. "Christ and Religious Pluralism," 543.

40. Clark H. Pinnock, "An Inclusivist View," in *Four Views on Salvation in a Pluralistic World*, 98.

41. "Being a Transformationist in a Pluralistic World," 749.

42. For a discussion on "conditional immortality" or annihilation, see *The Gagging of God*, 515–36.

43. Carl F. H. Henry, *Carl Henry at His Best: A Lifetime of Quotable Quotes* (Portland, Ore.: Multnomah, 1989), 209–10.

44. *The Gagging of God*, 27.

45. For examples of religious pluralists who understand the exclusivist message of the Scripture, yet adjust its application and meaning to fit their pluralist agenda, see Paul Schrotenboer, "Varieties of Pluralism," *Evangelical Review of Theology* 13, no. 2 (1989): 117.

### Chapter 7

1. Walter Bauer, *A Greek-English Lexicon of the New Testament and Other Early Christian Literature*, 2d ed., rev. F. Wilbur Gingrich and Frederick W. Danker, trans. William F Arndt and F. Wilber Gingrich (Chicago: University of Chicago Press, 1979), 98.

2. Liddell and Scott, *Greek English Lexicon*, 9th ed. (London: Oxford University Press, 1990), 218–19.

3. George Gunn and Edward Hindson, "Apostasy" in *The Dictionary of Premillennial Theology*, ed. Mal Couch (Grand Rapids: Kregel, 1996).

4. Charles C. Ryrie, *Dispensationalism*, rev. ed. (Chicago: Moody, 1995), 140.

5. Ibid.

6. Jaca Book, *The Church in the Age of Humanism* (Minneapolis: Winston, 1981), 43.

7. John Horsch, *Modern Religious Liberalism* (Chicago: The Bible Institute Colportage Association, 1938), 9.

8. Ibid., 26.

9. Ibid., 28.

10. Ibid.

11. Arthur Pink, foreword to *The Sovereignty of God* (Grand Rapids: Baker, 1992).

12. *Modern Religious Liberalism*, 220.

13. Mark Bleiweiss, "Slugged by an Angel," *Jewish Spectator* 63, no. 2 (fall 1998): 12.

14. Ibid., 14.

15. Ed Hindson, *Final Signs* (Eugene, Ore.: Harvest House, 1996), 189.

16. Faith Cook, *Grace in Winter* (Carlisle, Pa.: Banner of Truth, 1989), 75–76.

# COMING SOON
# FROM KREGEL

## The Fundamentals
## for the Twenty-First Century
*Examining the Crucial Issues of the Christian Faith*
Mal Couch, general editor
0-8254-2368-6

The evangelical faith that began this century with the publication of the historic work *The Fundamentals* finds itself once again challenged by cultural change and theological confusion.

This new collection, with chapters by over thirty evangelical scholars, examines contemporary biblical and social topics that affect every Christian's life and faith.

**Contributors include:**
Kerby Anderson • Paul Benware • Timothy Demy • Thomas Edgar • Paul Enns • Paul Fink • Harold Foos • Arnold Fruchtenbaum • Robert Gromacki • Gary Habermas • Edward Hindson • Henry Holloman • H. Wayne House • Thomas Ice • Tim LaHaye • Robert Lightner • Erwin Lutzer • Jobe Martin • Steve McAvoy • Thomas McCall • John McLean • George Meisinger • Henry Morris • David Noebel • Paige Patterson • Albert Platt • J. Randall Price • Gary Stewart • John Walvoord • Harold Willmington

**Topics include:**
abortion • attributes of God • Bible prophecy • the church • creation • eternity • ethics • evangelism • feminism • the family • inerrancy of the Bible • inspiration of Scripture • millennial kingdom • nature of salvation • pluralism • Satan and the spirit world • uniqueness of Christ